Moving Past the Past

A Guide for Adult Survivors of Childhood Sexual Abuse

Julie Poole
BSc; SQHP.

Copyright

Moving Past the Past: A Guide for Adult Survivors of Childhood Sexual Abuse
Text Copyright © 2017 Julie Poole

Moving Past the Past: A Guide for Adult Survivors of Childhood Sexual Abuse.
First Published 2017
Published by **J.P. Publishing**
Cover Design by Rebecca Poole from Dreams2Media
Formatting by Julie Poole
Editing by Julie Poole
Proofing by Harriette H. Charbonneau
ISBN 978-0-9933522-8-7

Special Thanks

I would like to thank the following people for their help with the development and production of this book:

Dreams2media - thank you Rebecca Poole for the fabulous book cover.

Hatsie - for your wonderful proofing and editing.
Helen – for your first proof. Pam for your second proof.
Michelle – for your invaluable advice on Revictimisation and yet another proof!

To my clients – for those I have worked with, helped, healed and learned from, and for those of you that have shared your stories here in this book that others may benefit from your own journey, thank you.

To my children, Tom, Chris, and Charlotte -- I love you all dearly and am grateful every day that you are part of my life.

To my readers - I thank you from the bottom of my heart for your support and kindness.

Finally, to all the survivors of childhood abuse – you are amazing!

Julie Poole

About the Author

Julie Poole is a Professional Hypnotherapist. She developed her Hypnotherapy practice in 2002 and has worked with over 2000 clients since, helping them to make the changes they seek. Most of her work's focus is predominantly around anxiety based issues, including sexual abuse and rape, physical and emotional abuse, death and loss, and more.

Julie specialises in working with clients who are experiencing issues due to their previous trauma and abuse. Many of her clients are not aware that their 'issue' is even linked to their abusive past! Symptoms which they present themselves to her with often include:

Depression, anxiety, anger, loss, insecurity, self-destructive patterns, overprotective parenting, jealousy and mistrust, obsessive compulsive disorder (OCD), post-traumatic stress disorder (PTSD), phobias, drug and alcohol abuse, food intolerances, chronic fatigue, fibromyalgia, addictions, migraines and relationship problems.

To specialise with working with survivors of abuse, and to help them to find a way forward has been a journey - a journey which she herself has made in order to heal from her own abuse.

Over time, Julie developed this mode of healing hypnotherapy further, working instinctively and intuitively with each client to bring them the same peace that she, her self has found. She has now helped hundreds of people who have experienced childhood sexual abuse to *Move Past their Past*, through working with her at her hypnotherapy practice. Some of her clients have willingly contributed their stories to this book, sharing with you how they themselves healed.

Julie is also the published author of three romantic comedy fiction books. Each contain elements of psychological growth and development, as well as spiritual and intuitive understanding weaved throughout the stories, details of which can be found on her author website:

Moving Past the Past: A Guide for Adult Survivors of Childhood Abuse is her first non-fiction, self-help book, and is based on her fifteen years' experience as a Hypnotherapist, her own experiences and those of working with hundreds of clients.

Julie trained and qualified as a Professional Hypnotherapist in 2002 obtaining a Diploma in Hypnotherapy (SAC Dip. Professional Hypnotherapy) and a Diploma in Regression Therapy (SAC Dip. Regression). She became registered with the GHR at that time – General Hypnotherapy Register (member number 1066), and the GHSC – General Hypnotherapy Standards Council. In October 2010 Julie was awarded SQHP from the GHR (which is a Senior Qualification in Hypnotherapy Practice status) due to her experience and professional development. In February 2015 she became a full member of the CNCH (Complimentary and Natural Healthcare Council) – registration number 000106-B15. In 2017, after four years of studying for a degree in psychology and sociology, Julie Poole obtained a Batchelor of Science.

Dedication

***

I have been amazed and astounded by the changes that my clients have made to their lives through hypnotherapy sessions with me over the past fifteen years. I consider myself blessed to have been a part of each person's journey; a journey which is often challenging – taking trust, determination and a willingness to overcome their individual obstacles in order to find the release and peace that each seeks. I am proud to have known and worked with each and every one of them.

This book is dedicated to you

***

Contents

Introduction

If you're reading this book, welcome! To understand the impact that childhood sexual abuse has on the adult is not an easy journey to make, but one which will, I hope, help you to finally *Move Past the Past*.

For the partners of survivors, or for the parents and family of survivors, this book is for you too.

Moving Past the Past will help you to understand yourself (or your partner, child, sister or brother) in a way that you never thought possible. It will show you why you (they) behave 'like that,' and why you (they) react 'like that.' It will show you what the triggers are that create those reactions and help you to understand them. For the adult survivors of childhood sexual abuse who experience these reactions, it will show you how you can release and overcome them.

Many survivors find a lifetime of chaos, broken relationships, multiple jobs, multiple homes, destructiveness, insecurity and illness (physical, mental and emotional.) My hope for you is that this book will help you with *Moving Past the Past* and into security, stability, wellness, inner peace and tranquillity; to strengthen your relationships with yourself, and with others, and to move towards a peaceful and stable life.

What's in a name? Many object to the term 'survivor,' others object to the term 'victim.' If you are still reacting, suffering and responding to your childhood abuse, then I believe that you are still a 'victim' of that abuse. Once that reaction has gone, you may consider yourself to be a 'survivor.' For now, throughout this book, I will refer to us as, 'Survivors.' Whichever term you prefer, the aim of this book is to get you to the point in your life where you are neither – the name, label or definition will be irrelevant, no longer important; you are simply someone who experienced childhood sexual abuse long ago.

For us to make changes we need first to understand - understanding is the key! To understand *why* we do what we do is the first step to being able to change the old patterns, reactions, responses and triggers. The journey throughout this book will help you to do just this. It is filled with studies, information, explanations, and other people's stories, as well as exercises for you to follow.

The studies and other references are numbered. You will find the full list of them in the Bibliography section at the end of the book.

It is my hope for you that this book will help you to find your way through the maze of destruction that being an 'adult survivor of childhood sexual abuse' often brings; to let it go, to find your way out of the cycle of despair and destruction, and to finally be able to *Move Past the Past*.

Now, shall we get started?

Chapter 1 - You are stronger than you know

You are strong! Did you know this? Perhaps you feel anything *but* strong – weak, vulnerable, chaotic, depressed, hopeless, inadequate, stupid... the list goes on, but, you *are* strong, *very* strong! You are stronger than you know. For a start, you're still here! Right here on Planet Earth, reading this book, right here, right now. This, in itself, is an enormous achievement. Do you have any idea how many others did not survive? No, nor me! Trying to obtain figures about the amount of suicides with a history or background of Childhood Sexual Abuse doesn't seem to exist. Why? I'd like to know how many others didn't make it, didn't get this far; how many of us 'victims' never made it to 'survivor' status. What are the figures and statistics to getting past the age of twenty-five and still being alive for those like us? Well, what I have found is that adults over twenty-five with Childhood Sexual Abuse are twice as likely to attempt suicide as those that have not experienced Childhood Sexual Abuse.[1] Twice as likely is a lot! But, it's a lot better than ten times more likely! It seems the older you are, the more likely you are to make it. It's that crucial time, thirteen to twenty-five that seems to be the highest risk time, with a suicide rate of ten times the national average. Roughly a third of all sexually abused children have attempted suicide, and 43% have thought about it.[2] How many of those didn't make it we may never know. They aren't here to tell us what happened, why they did it, why they didn't want to live any more. Were they abused? Sadly, it's highly likely. Did you know that 70% of all psychiatric emergency room patients report a history of childhood physical or sexual abuse?[3] (These are the people that are sectioned or enter voluntarily into a psychiatric unit because they are actively suicidal.) Grim reading isn't it? So, you see, the odds have been stacked against us for most of our life, and yet, we're still here. Somehow, we have survived, battled through and made a life for ourselves. But what kind of life is it?

Let's have a look at some detail of this thing called Childhood Sexual Abuse (which I will call CSA from now on), and its effects and affects. Now, I know this is hard reading, but please bear with me. We have spent a lifetime turning away from our past, pushing it down, ignoring, repressing, suppressing, and denying . . . has it worked? I would assume not, or you'd be unlikely to be here, reading this book on how to get past it. Trust me on this; the more you can understand this terrible thing we have experienced, the easier it is to overcome it. The rest of this Chapter is going to explain much more about CSA than you ever wanted to know, but try to read on if you can. If you can't, skip to Chapter 2, when the healing journey begins.

So, let's start at the beginning. What is CSA? The definition is broader than most people think. CSA includes any sexual act between an adult and a minor, or between two minors, when one exerts power over the other. That may include forcing, coercing or persuading a child to engage in any type of sexual act as well as non-contact acts, such as exhibitionism, exposure to pornography, voyeurism, and communicating in a sexual manner by phone or Internet.

In my opinion, one of the worst feelings of CSA (of the many) is this sense that you are alone. The isolation is palpable at times. The sense of being different, not part of, outside of... I know! We all do. But, we are not alone, sadly. Across the world, 20% of children have been sexually abused. In the US, 16% of men and 26% of women have been sexually abused in childhood.[4] According to the NSPCC, 5% of children in the UK have been sexually abused.[5] (However, most studies put the figure higher, at around 10%, and those are just the reported cases.)

How much damage can one sex offender do? Well on average, one perpetrator will molest an average of 120 victims, most of whom do not report it, and 90% of perpetrators abuse children that they know.[6] There is a lot of us out there, so, that's step 1 – stop feeling alone. You're not!

Studies began in the 1990s, looking at the effects of CSA on long term health. The most famous study is the 'ACE' study.[7] It is well worth having a look at this, as it will really help you to get a better understanding of who you are. A simple 'Google' search of ACE will bring you up all sorts, but Wiki is a good place to find what you need. (There are also all the references at the end of this book for the articles, studies and sites that I have taken these figures and statistics from.) Basically, the 'ACE' study examined the relationship between health in adulthood and previous exposure to emotional, physical, or sexual abuse, and other household dysfunction during childhood. It came up with ten indicators (events), which are; Physical abuse; Sexual abuse; Emotional abuse; Physical neglect; Emotional neglect; Mother treated violently; Household substance abuse; Household mental illness; Parental separation or divorce; Incarcerated household member.

The outcome from the study found that the more of these events that you have experienced, the more likely that you are to have issues with health in adulthood.

Do a quick count now, how many of those did you have? I have 8 out of 10. Yep, it wasn't great, my childhood! My parents split when I was seven or eight, although Dad worked away a lot before that. Mum couldn't cope after he went and went into a deep depression, hitting the bottle hard. She also hit Valium, sleeping pills, uppers, downers and anything else that she could legally get her hands on, in her attempts to avoid the pain. Mum also regularly 'lost it' in terms of screaming at us, hitting us, verbally/emotionally abusing us, and eventually, she broke down completely. She was sectioned into a psychiatric unit where she spent some months as a resident, followed by, I think, two years as an outpatient. At the point of sectioning, I had, thankfully, been removed to the relative safety of my father's house a few months before. My elder brother had escaped too, off to university, leaving my older sister, just sixteen at the time, to deal with it all on her own.

During those turbulent four years, in the mix of abuse, neglect, loneliness and fear, I became the prime target for the local neighbourhood paedophile; being groomed beautifully over several months into sexual abuse and eventual rape at around the age of eight. (Like many of us, the detail of my exact age during this grooming and abuse is vague.) By the time I was eleven years old, I was totally 'off the rails,' displaying behaviour of trauma (anger, defiance, disobedience), and was regularly in trouble at both school and at home, with grades and education slipping into an abyss. Sound familiar?

My abuser was a neighbour, and my abuse included physical penetration. Studies show that abuse involving either physical penetration and/or abuse involving a father or stepfather has greater long-term harm.[8] This doesn't in any way diminish abuse without penetration, or from non-parental family members, but the clinical studies demonstrate that the long term affects have a more destructive force, often leading onto more severe destruction, such as substance abuse, eating disorders, suicide and self-harm. We are also far more likely to develop anxiety disorders, particularly post-traumatic stress disorder (PTSD), and even experience psychotic symptoms.[9]

Now, let's talk about the head, and, in particular the brain. Don't panic, I'm not going to get all medical on you. That being said, did you know that your CSA has programmed your brain to be on constant danger alert? Did you know that? I didn't! Not until I recently studied psychology and sociology for my degree did I even know they existed. So, let me explain. There is a part of your brain called the 'Amygdala' and another called the 'Hippocampus.' These two centres are in what is called the 'limbic system,' which is our emotional brain. They are responsible for all emotion and in particular, memory and fear. Studies have shown that CSA creates abnormalities in these areas and predispose the person to high levels of impulsivity, impaired decision making and suicidal behaviour. Your brain has got wired to fear life and to make bad decisions! It's not your fault. Did you hear me? **It's not your fault!** (You'll hear me say this a lot throughout this book – It's not your fault!)

"Can this programming be changed after all this time?" I hear you ask. Yes, thank God, it can. Later on in this book, we will do some exercises to begin the reprogramming.

Now, let's talk about, 'Feeling/being thick!' Academic problems in childhood are a common symptom of sexual abuse. Did you know that sexually abused children perform lower on psychometric tests measuring cognitive ability, academic achievement and memory assessments? Studies indicate that sexual abuse exposure among children and adolescents is linked with high-school absentee rates, special education services and academic difficulties. In fact, a history of CSA significantly increases the chance of dropping out of school altogether.

So, you dropped out? Yep, me too! I was top of my class for years, on the road to university, but it all became too much and I dropped out at sixteen, failing all but two of my nine 'O' levels ('O' levels are the 'olden days' GCSE's for you 'youngsters' reading this). Did you, like me, decide there and then that you were a failure, doomed for unemployment? Did you go from dead-end job to dead-end job for years? Or did you go the other way – high achiever, always striving for more in an effort to prove to the world that you're not quite as rubbish as you feel? Or did you go on benefits and into unemployment? Me, I went into motherhood; pregnant within four months of leaving school. I quickly married a man almost as damaged as I was and spent the next five years living in total dysfunction and chaos, adding more abuse to my broken spirit, along with two miscarriages.

All that is the negative stuff, so let's look at the positive. After five years of chaos, I was by then divorced, and met a new, stable and kind man. I got married again, had another child and then started to rebuild me. A few years on, and I went back to college at the age of twenty-eight, studied for four years and qualified in my chosen profession at the time, housing management. I forged a career in housing, support and homelessness; a career I became quite successful in. Ten years later, I studied again, this time, for my hypnotherapy diplomas. Another ten years on, and I finally did it! I enrolled in university at the age of fifty and, at the age of fifty-four I shall be collecting my degree, finally! See, it's never too late! So, no matter what your education, what your academic achievements, you are not thick, you are not stupid, you are not a failure. Do not write yourself off! The CSA you experienced put the spokes in your education, but that does not mean you are thick! Neither does it mean that it is forever.

Now, let's talk about alcohol and drugs. Wonderful anaesthetics aren't they? Numb that pain right down! Can't feel a thing? Excellent! Well, not really – it's just delaying the inevitable, plus adding something else destructive that you have to deal with later, into that already damaged soul. A number of studies have found that adolescents with a history of CSA demonstrate a three to fourfold increase in rates of substance abuse/dependence.[10] Something else we need to recover from then, plus the CSA that led us there in the first place!

What about food? That's a substance too! It's something else for us to abuse in our self-destruction patterns. Obesity and eating disorders are far more common in women who have a history of

CSA. Figures show that sixteen to twenty-four year-old women with CSA are four times more likely than their non-abused peers to be diagnosed with an eating disorder.[11] And, middle-aged women who were sexually abused as children are twice as likely to be obese.[12]

Let us now look at health, and the impact of CSA on our health. That is, after all, why the ACE study was conducted in the first place. So, what did it find? Generally, adult victims of CSA have higher rates of health problems and report significantly more health complaints, compared to adults without a child sexual abuse history. Adult survivors of CSA are at greater risk of a wide range of conditions, including fibromyalgia, severe premenstrual syndrome, chronic headaches, irritable bowel syndrome and a wide range of reproductive and sexual health complaints, including excessive bleeding, pain during intercourse and menstrual irregularity.

Not only do we have more minor health conditions, but we are at greater risk for the more serious conditions as well. We are 30% more likely to have a serious medical condition such as diabetes, cancer, heart problems, stroke or hypertension. Male CSA survivors have twice the HIV-infection rate of non-abused males. In a study of HIV infected twelve to twenty year olds, 41% reported a sexual abuse history.

What else do we know? According to the NSPCC, CSA costs the UK £3.2 billion a year. Wow! It's an expensive business, being damaged, isn't it! Feel bad? Don't! We've already got enough on our enormous plate of guilt without taking on anymore! Oh, I said the 'G' word! I didn't mean to come onto that right now, as, let's be fair, it's huge! We'll do that 'biggy' later. In the meantime, let's talk 'psychology'.

We survivors of CSA often have feelings of isolation and stigma, as well as dreadfully poor self-esteem. Oftentimes, this leads to suicidal behaviour, thoughts and actions when these are reactivated and triggered by similar situations in adulthood. Let me explain what I mean by this. As children and teenagers, we feel dirty, disgusting, not worthy, full of self-blame, lonely, unloved and uncared for. We are desperate for love and affection, validation and worth. We will do almost anything to get it! It drives us at our core - this 'need' to be accepted, loved, cared for, and to feel safe. And we find it, for a while! And then it's gone, and we crash, and we crash big time! The relationship that made us feel whole (for a while) has gone, and we are not only now back to where we were before, but worse – we can now add on another rejection, another loss of trust, and, we can often (sadly), add on another lot of abuse (physical, mental, sexual, emotional), to go on top of what we are already carrying. The load gets heavier with each failed relationship, with each failed job, with each failed . . . (Fill in the blanks.) Now add on a few addictions, some mental health issues, a few tantrums or melt-downs, and what have you got? Me? You? Ah, the damage my dears, could we ever have imagined?

Most of us have spent our lives running from it, totally unaware why our lives are such a disaster. I know I did. Not a clue had I! I was thirty-seven, coming out of another failed relationship, another move of home, unable to cope with the pressure or stress of my, by then, successful career (we don't do stress well, you know!), and I had no clue why I was the way I was. "What is wrong with me?" I often asked myself. "Why can't I get it together?" I had suffered bouts of depression and anxiety on and off throughout my entire life, and, no matter how successful I was or how happy I was in a relationship, I couldn't sustain anything for long, and the depression would come back. Nothing lasted, and each failure saw my tiny ego, esteem and confidence dented and shrink even more. Even my beautiful children couldn't be enough to hold my fragile, broken spirit together, despite the love between us.

Anyways, I digress. So, finally, let's now look at what this 'CSA', this 'abuse' is.

"I know what it is!" I hear you shout. Yes, you do. You know *your* abuse. Do you know and understand others? Maybe you have had one of these, or maybe your abuse has been a combination of several of them. Let me share with you what I know . . . (And, by the way, I don't pretend to know everything!)

One of the most confusing areas of CSA for many is what is known as 'Grooming.' This is a totally different type of abuse to that of being attacked. I have heard people ask, "Why didn't he/ she scream, or fight, or yell? Why didn't he/she tell? Why did he/she keep going back?" There is a real lack of understanding on this one, and I want to try to dispel some of it. There are different types of abuse; they are not all the same, they are different, and, they have different impacts and different traumas on the victims. Let's spend a bit of time looking at these different types of abuse.

Stranger abuse – these attacks often come out of the blue. The child is dragged into a bush, van, park, house or other place and sexually assaulted, molested and/or raped. The attack may also happen in a friends' house. The attacker may be the father, visitor or relative of the friend. It is generally a one-time incident, extremely traumatic and results in huge shock for the child, PTSD and more. The child is more likely to tell their parents in this type of abuse, but not always. If the child does tell, the parents are usually out of their mind with grief, hugely supportive of, and to, the child. The Police are often involved and are also, usually, supportive. They involve victim support, counselling and child psychology. The child is, hopefully, given every opportunity to heal, work through and to deal with their abuse. The event will stay with them for life, but they are often able to function in adulthood well, despite the incident, because of the love and support around them at the time. Having a low ACE score (home is not dysfunctional) makes a significant difference on their ability to move past this trauma.

Family incest – The most common form of sexual abuse, incest is carried out by a parent, step-parent, brother, uncle, grandfather or other family member. The breach of trust to the child is indescribable, and often results in the complete inability to trust anyone or anything, or to develop real intimacy or emotional bonding with another human being. When we experience this type of CSA, we don't trust our own perceptions and we become an expert in disbelieving our own senses. We try to convince ourselves that we over-reacted and that nothing really terrible happened: "My daddy would never *really* hurt me." Ah, denial, isn't it powerful? Family incest, particularly by a father or step-father has been found to have the highest levels of long-term damage in adult survivors of CSA. In terms of risk, children who live with a single parent that have a live-in partner are at the highest risk of all - they are 20 times more likely to be victims of child sexual abuse than children living with both biological parents.[13] This type of abuse is rarely reported, and the Police are rarely involved.

Abuses by other children – 40% of abused children are abused by other children, not adults.[14]

Grooming - Abusers often form close relationships with potential victims and/or their families prior to the abuse. This is called "grooming." Grooming is a process where the offender gradually draws the victim into a sexual relationship and maintains that relationship in secrecy. At the same time, the offender may also fill roles within the victim's family that make the offender trusted and valued, such as a friend, babysitter or carer.

Grooming behaviours often include special attention, outings, and gifts. The offender works hard to firstly identify and then meet the child's unmet needs, with lots of affection, attention, play and cuddles, actively targeting children with high ACE scores.[15] (They seem to be able to spot a vulnerable, neglected child at twenty paces! How, I have no idea, but they do.) They are smart, quick, sly and clever. The bond they build with the family means that it is very difficult for the child to tell, as they assume that no one would believe them. (That's assuming that they even realise that they have been abused, because most do not.) Let me explain . . .

These types of perpetrators are often highly organised, intelligent, manipulative and controlling. They will treat the child as if he or she is older, encouraging them to be 'grown up,' gradually crossing physical boundaries, and becoming increasingly sexual. The child will often grow to love this person, and believe that they are, 'in a relationship with,' the perpetrator. They are usually unaware that they are being abused at all! Why? They are being brainwashed and programmed to believe that the sexual actions are normal and acceptable between them and their abuser. This is a type of abuse (to my knowledge, and in my experience) where the child will enjoy some of the sexual activity, and often responds in a sexual manner to the touch, given enough time. This type of abuse leaves particular scars of self-blame, self-disgust and shame. They 'loved' the abuser, they remember often enjoying the sexual part, and cannot believe the abuser would hurt them, or that the abuser did anything wrong. It leaves immense confusion in the child, which plays out in adulthood. Again, this type of abuse is rarely reported.

Short-term and long-term abuse – for some, their abuse is one single occasion. For others, it is a handful of occasions. For others it is over a period of months, but for some, it is years. It is not unusual for me to work with a client who has been the victim of CSA from the age of four right up to fifteen, experiencing abuse on a daily or weekly basis for all those years. At that time (fourteen to sixteen years of age), the survivor will find a way out of the cycle of abuse, often by leaving home, moving in with a partner, running away, and, at a last resort, by committing suicide. Studies show that the longer the length of time that the abuse goes on for, the more damage it does to the person on every level.

Scary bit coming - I have never, in all my fifteen years of working in this field, had a single client who reported their abuse to the police, including myself. We are the silent majority. I did though, tell my father, but only at the age of forty, when I was going through my own healing. His response - I have a vivid imagination, it couldn't have happened, it's impossible! Okay then! Now, we are dealing with our parents' denial, as well as our own. How many others did tell someone and weren't believed either? Is that the ultimate betrayal? I think it is. Many of my clients told their mum, or their dad, and weren't believed. Heart breaking, isn't it?

As we can see, there are many types of childhood sexual abuse, and just as many different types of perpetrators, each leaving their own type of scars. It's estimated that 38% of victims never disclose their abuse. (I, personally, think it's much higher.)[16] Of those that do, of all the total reported cases of sexual assault of all ages, 70% are assaults on children under seven years old. Of all reported rapes, 40% of those are also on children.

The types of abuse that I have listed here are the ones that I am aware of and have worked with. I know there are many more. It is important to find out more about your type of abuse in order to understand some of your drives and motivations, fears and actions. The more you know, the easier and quicker it is to heal and release them. When you've finished this Chapter, please take a little time to do some research, google some abuse organisations, find out a little more from the 'official experts,' like Psychologists, Psychiatrists, Sexual Abuse Counsellors, charity organisations etc.. I am none of these things; I am a Hypnotherapist with a lot of experience, both personally and professionally, but I am not an official expert. Find out as much as you can, because the knowledge creates the understanding, and the understanding starts the healing process.

Now, I know this Chapter has been terribly depressing reading - all these facts and figures, and I agree, it is! You may have experienced depression, had suicide attempts, had mental health problems, drug or alcohol problems, been arrested, convicted, been in prison, been promiscuous, been a sex worker, have no education, feel thick, not good enough, not worthy. You are not alone, and now that you have read all these facts and figures, you can begin to see that your destructive behaviour is actually a 'normal' response to what you've been through, rather than an 'abnormal' one. You may have previously felt that you are a waste of space, a slight on society. Don't! You may have been ashamed of your past actions and behaviours, you may regret them, that's ok! I regret many of mine! But, you literally were not in your right mind when you made those mistakes, when you carried out those destructive actions. You literally couldn't have been any other way - *then*. But, as you begin to understand just how much you have suffered, why you suffer, why you act this way and why you continue to suffer, only then will you finally realise just how strong you are. And you are! Do you see it now? Do you see that this is not your fault, do you see that you are strong? And you need that strength to heal, because facing up to your abuse and releasing all that pain inside you is going to be hard at times.

Your instinct will be to keep avoiding, keep running, keep searching for distractions, and I am asking you to stop. STOP! STOP! STOP! You can't run, you can't hide: it is inside you. No relationship, no job, no money, no distraction can make this go away. It just puts a temporary plaster over the gaping wound; a wound that continues to fester and leak toxic pain into you every hour of every day. No matter where you go or how fast you run, it is with you. It will always be with you - until you stop, stand still and let it catch you. You turn and slowly face it, and you stand strong. You look your demons right in the eye, and you say, "Bring it on! I am ready! It is time!"

This is the beginning of your journey into wholeness, a journey to bring the broken bits of you back together. It is a journey to reprogramme your wiring, your beliefs and your drives . . . a journey to release your disgust, your shame and your pain . . . a journey to feel clean enough, good enough, worthy, lovable, deserving . . . a journey into peace where you can *Move Past the Past* once and for all. Come with me now on that journey. I will hold your hand all the way through it, I promise. You are not alone and you are strong. Ready?

Chapter 2 - Why me?

Why me? Ah the victim! We do get stuck in that rut don't we? We can be very good at feeling sorry for ourselves, and this is okay - it's allowed. Did you think I would tell you off? Don't be daft! We *should* feel sorry for ourselves! We had it hard, we suffered. It isn't right and it isn't fair that we had those experiences, and we absolutely should put sympathy, love and care into ourselves. But are we? Is that what we are doing, or are we just wallowing in how shit life is? (Excuse the language here, but we need to get real.) Do you think that life is something that happens to you, that everything always goes wrong, that life is a bitch? Dichotomy isn't it, because so far, life has been a bitch! But, as long as we stay in that attitude, it always will be.

So, here's my take on it . . . Life is hard, problems happen, things go wrong. Let's accept that as a fact, because if we are waiting for the charmed life, the perfect life, we missed the train. Life is hard. Full stop. What now?

Now? Now, we look at responsibility. I know! Confusing isn't it? I tell you that, "It is not your fault," and then I say, "Take responsibility!"

Let me explain . . .

The abuse was not your fault. Your reactions to it were not your fault – and yes, that includes all those bad decisions, all that bad behaviour, reactive behaviour, poor choices, etc., etc. They were your programmes, your beliefs and they drove you. Look back now at your past, with all its chaos, destruction and mess, and say right now,

"None of that was my fault."

I could go on here to say, "Now forgive yourself."

But. . . I won't.

Why?

Because there is nothing to forgive.

The End.

That was then, all those mistakes, all those bad choices, all that abuse. Then! But . . . This is now.

It was not your fault, *because you didn't know, because you couldn't help it.* How can we take responsibility for things we didn't know we were doing, things that we weren't aware of and couldn't have controlled? We couldn't! But, now that we are starting to become aware of them, now we can start to do something about them, and that begins with taking responsibility.

From this point forward, you, and only you, are taking responsibility for your healing. Only you can heal you. I can help, so can many others, but I can't do it for you, no one can. *You* have to do this. You have to *want* to do this; to want to change, to want a better life, to want an easier life. And you do, and I know you do, or you wouldn't be reading this!

The first thing we take responsibility for is our mirror. Aye? Yes, mirror. Life is a mirror. It reflects back to you, in its pictures, the inner you. If you don't like the view in the mirror, don't smash the mirror (we've tried that, didn't work did it?). Let's change the inner me so that we can get a nicer reflection back. Let me explain . . .

You meet a lovely man/woman; very loving, affectionate and charming. You begin a relationship with him/her. Before long, he/she starts to be unreliable, disrespectful, controlling, etc.

"Why me?" you lament. "Why do I always attract the crap ones?"

Well, that's your mirror, Hun. If you want someone to treat you with kindness, to honour you, to respect you, to really love you unconditionally, to value you, to trust you, to be trustworthy, to love all of you (warts and all), you have to do, and be, exactly the same to you. To you, not to them! Oh my goodness, we are SO good at pouring love onto others, aren't we? Then we sit back and wonder what we did wrong, and why they don't love us back the way we loved them; why they don't treat us right - we treated them right! Now, it's really important that you get this bit, really get it.

The mirror is not a reflection of the way you treat others. It's a reflection of the way you treat you!

If you want the mirror to change, you have to start loving you, properly. Then, and only then, will someone come into your life who will love you the way you want to be loved.

Now, I have used the example here of a relationship. It can be, and is, everything! Not just relationships, but jobs, homes, friends, children, plans, arrangements, everything!

Plans? What do I mean by plans?

You make arrangements to go for dinner – the restaurant loses your booking. "So unreliable!" you huff.

You make plans to go on holiday – you lose your passport, the car breaks down, etc. "Bloody useless car!" you huff. "Damned passport is hiding from me!"

In the past you would probably have lamented,

"Why me? Why does everything go wrong for me?"

And you are back in the 'woe is me' pity party, back in victim mode - angry, confused, disappointed and more.

It went wrong because it reflects back to you the way you are with you. Do you let yourself down? Promise yourself something then not do it? Are you unreliable with yourself? Do you trust yourself, do you listen to yourself, or do you ignore your inner voice, inner needs, desires and wants? If you let yourself down, others will, too. If you don't trust yourself, you will attract people who are untrustworthy. If you attract insecure people, it reflects back to you your own insecurity. If you are ignoring you, life will reflect that back, and you will find that people ignore you, too. And we hate that, don't we? We hate being ignored! Do you know why?

Being ignored is a massive trigger back to the childhood trauma. It tugs on the pain and it comes flooding up. All of a sudden we are having a very bad reaction. Some will say it's an over-reaction, and it is, in a way. You are reacting to the situation, but you are adding the old hurt to it, so it is bigger than it should be for the thing today that triggered it.

Being ignored makes us feel invisible, and we know that one, don't we? The abuse happened probably because of neglecting parents, absent parents, no parents, too trusting parents, unaware parents, blind, blinkered parents, drunk parents, etc.

"Why didn't they see, why didn't they notice, why didn't someone save me?"

Feel invisible? You should, because you were. How can you be so invisible? How can adults who are meant to care and protect you miss so many, very obvious signs?

Child sexual abuse victims often exhibit indirect physical signs, such as anxiety, chronic stomach pain and headaches.[17] Emotional and behavioural signals are common among sexually abused children. Some of these are 'too perfect' behaviours, withdrawal, fear, depression, unexplained anger and rebellion. Some common consequences of trauma include nightmares, bedwetting, falling grades, cruelty to animals, bullying, being bullied, fire setting, runaway, and self-harm of any kind.[18] One of the most telling signs that sexual abuse is occurring, is sexual behaviour and language that is not age appropriate.[19]

I don't know about you, but I displayed most of those signs from about the age of eight. No one noticed! Not a single person. Not my mother, my brother, my sister, my teachers, my friends' parents; no one! Why? Inside we are screaming, "Notice! Help me!" but no one does. Outside, we are acting up, acting out, screaming to get noticed, but no one does. We didn't get rescued, we didn't get help, and we didn't get noticed. We were invisible.

Even when I managed to down every bottle of my mothers' pills on a forced visit back to her for half term, in my first suicide attempt at the tender age of twelve or thirteen, no one noticed. Oh, they noticed the overdose, don't get me wrong. I was whipped into hospital for a stomach pump quick smart, and then whipped home again quickly, back to my fathers' house the next day, where I was firmly told,

"We will not speak of this again, ever!"

I am sure I heard him say to my step-mum as he left my bedroom door, "What an embarrassment this would be, if it ever got out!"

I was an embarrassment, an inconvenience, a drama queen, I was vying for attention.

"Attention seeking behaviour" was a term that was bandied about quite a lot throughout my childhood by my father. This overdose was another one of those inconvenient dramas, and one which I was forbidden to discuss, ever again. And it wasn't.

That had been the moment; the moment for help, the moment that was missed, the opportunity for the blinkers to come off, for the rescue squad to come sweeping in - but it didn't. I distinctly recall the doctor at the hospital, as he was discharging me to my aunt's care (she was my taxi, collecting me and returning me to my fathers' house – he, as always, was too busy, and my mother was 'too traumatised' from my overdose to be able to come), telling her that he strongly recommended that immediate psychiatric help be accessed as I clearly had some deep, underlying issues that needed to be explored. The instructions were not followed and nothing was explored. In my family, it was simply brushed under the carpet.

Does this ring true for you? Do you resonate with this 'invisible' thing?

So, how can we fix that feeling of being invisible? We can't go back and change the past, make someone notice, or make someone care. We are not Doctor Who, riding back into the past in our very own Tardis on a rescue mission. Well, actually, yes we can. We can't change the event, we can't stop the abuse from happening, but we can go back. We can go back to that 'little me' (I call mine, 'Mini-Me'), and, we can listen.

So, here is your first exercise to begin the healing.

Before you do this, make sure that you will be undisturbed as much as possible. Pick a quiet time; turn off phones, door bell and other distractions. Get a box of tissues ready in case you cry. Have a glass of water for after too, as you may well be thirsty.

Exercise 1- Meeting 'Mini-Me'

Close your eyes and take a few deep breaths. Allow your body to relax. Imagine that you are breathing in a beautiful, misty light which is filled with peace, tranquillity and safety, and imagine it going deeply into you. Give it a colour, any colour that comes to you in that moment. Allow it to swirl around your body, into your body, feel it spreading through you, and with each breath, you are relaxing deeper, easier.

Imagine it filling your mind, your thoughts, and everything going quiet.

Now, imagine a door to a beautiful garden. Go through the door, step onto the grass, listen to the birds singing, smell the fragrance of the flowers, hear the water trickle in the nearby lake, feel the sun shining down warmly on your back. Have a walk around, explore. There are benches and chairs dotted around, little paths meandering through the garden. Take your time, and when you are ready, pick a place that feels right to you and sit down.

Imagine coming into the garden towards you, is 'Little You,' your own Mini-Me.

Now, invite him/her to sit down next to you. Introduce yourself. Tell him/her who you are. You might say something like,

"Hi. I'm you from the future. I've come back to help you. I'm all grown up now. I'm safe, I'm strong; we made it."

Now, encourage Mini-Me to talk to you. You are their new best friend, their mentor, their protector, all rolled into one. From this moment forward, you are there to protect Mini-Me, to stick up for him/her, to listen to him/her, and above all, to care for him/her. I want you to love this child, deeply, fully, unconditionally. Look at him/her. See their little face, see their sad eyes, see their pain, see *them*. Hold them, cuddle them, let them cry, let them vent. Let them do whatever they need to do. Mini-Me is no longer invisible. He/she has you now and you will hear, support and care for him/her. You will understand this little person in a way that no one ever has, because Mini-Me is you!

Whilst you do this exercise, you may feel very emotional. That's fine, it's safe, and it's okay. Have a good cry.

Understand that Mini-Me lives inside you. Imagine him/her stepping back into you, into the safety of you. You are like a Russian Doll – you know the ones that all fit inside each other, getting smaller and smaller? This is you. The outer you, the 'you' that you see in the mirror every day, well that's the biggest one. How many smaller ones do you have living inside you? How many of them are crying? Precisely! How can you ever be happy until all of your 'you's' are happy? Each and every one of your Mini-Me's needs to be listened to, fixed, repaired and restored. This is your mission.

I want you to meet with your Mini-Me every day, and to check in on him/her, just like a really caring best friend. Allow other Mini-Me's to come forward, too. Allow them to bond with you, and with each other. Help them to feel safe, loved, worthy and good enough. Wash away their tears, their sorrow and take away their fear. Keep reassuring them that they are safe now.

(If you struggle with visualising, you may find it helpful to download my audio self-hypnosis on this. Recovering from Childhood Sexual Abuse which you can find on my website, and which includes a visualisation of meeting Mini-Me.)

Gradually, the Mini-Me's become bigger Mini-Me's, moving up from the little you (age two to twelve), then into teens (thirteen to sixteen), then the young adult (sixteen to twenty-five), then the more grown up parts of yourselves that are lost and damaged from your twenties, thirties etc. Keep going up until the present day, until they are all feeling safe, valued, appreciated, cared for and above all, heard!

The exercise you just did is called 'inner child' work, and is an absolutely essential part of healing you.

I must say here, that one of my clients could not find his Mini-Me. He did, however, see a cat in the garden during his visualisation. The cat was high up on a wall watching him, and wouldn't come near him. It was feral, fiercely independent, untrusting and wary. This is the way his Mini-Me showed itself, as a cat, not as the seven-year-old abused child. My client imagined himself sat on a blanket in the garden, lit a camp fire, and stayed put for hours, until the sun went down. He placed a second blanket near the fire on the opposite side of the fire (for the cat) and a bowl of food and water. The cat stayed put on the wall, watching him. My client watched the flames flicker on his camp fire, watched the cat through the light of the moon that filled the garden, and eventually, with patience, the cat approached him. It still wouldn't let him touch it, but it did curl up by the fire on the blanket, and ate some of the food. It was wary, but was showing that it was willing to trust him, a little.

My client did not give up. He kept going back to the garden in many more visualisations over the following weeks, and, in time, the cat came a little closer, until eventually, it curled up on his lap and snuggled him.

For myself, I also could not find my Mini-Me on my first visit. It took me several attempts. I kept the intention, sending out love to 'little me' across the garden, calling for her, reassuring her that I was there to help. Eventually, I noticed a door. I think it was in a tree trunk! I opened the door and could see these dark, steep, stone steps leading down. The smell was disgusting, but I felt drawn to go down the steps. They were kind of carved into the stone wall, and it felt like I was going down into a deep, dark dungeon. When I got to the bottom, that's exactly what it was! There she was, at the bottom of this dungeon - filthy dirty and up to her waist in about three feet of raw sewerage. She was covered in it! Her hair was matted, filth ingrained into her scrawny face, sewerage over her whole body, and this is where she lived, and had been living, forever. She was seven years old! I called out to her and she shrank back against the far wall, telling me not to come any nearer, because she didn't want to contaminate me, to make me dirty and smelly like her. There was no hesitation, I wasn't going to leave her there! I stepped down and into the sewerage and waded over to her, wrapped her in my arms, and held her. She struggled a lot, but I just kept reassuring her that she was safe, that I wasn't going to let her go, that I was there to help, and that I wasn't leaving this dungeon without her. I asked her to trust me. She begged me to leave her there, where no one could see her filth or her shame. I kept reassuring. I told her that the garden, 'up there,' at the top of the steps, was beautiful. I told her that it was time, that she was safe, and that I loved her. In time, she stopped struggling and let me carry her up the steps. We came out of the darkness and into the light, and she looked down at herself and her filth with shame. She looked at the mess on me (that had rubbed off from her) and she began to cry. I told her not to worry, that it didn't matter, and then I took her to the lake. I took her into its healing, cleansing waters, and I washed her clean. We were there a while! As we stepped out of the lake, she transformed from the filthy rags she'd been found in; now wearing a beautiful white dress with blue ribbons in her hair - and she smiled. It was her first smile for thirty years! We sat together on the bench and we talked, and cuddled, and eventually, we played.

She now lives in the garden, plays on the swing that hangs from one of the trees, or with her many pets (she has a Unicorn!) and she comes to see me often. She also has other people now to play with, the other 'Mini-Me's' of ten, twelve and fifteen years of age. Sometimes she wants to step into me and be with me, other times she wants to stay and play in the garden. I let her do whatever she wants to do.

Mini-Me felt so dirty and disgusting inside, that the image she had of herself outside was reflected with the dungeon and sewerage. In her mind, she deserved to live in this dungeon, in the 'shit,' because that was what she was - filth! Bless her! No wonder I'd had a job sorting out my self-esteem and worth when inner me felt so dirty. Not only had I not had self-love, it was total self-hatred! I'd had no idea that all of that was inside me, until I opened up Pandora's Box and looked. After this, my self-esteem and self-love began to grow. No longer feeling dirty, deep in my core, the light began to shine. The sun, literally, came out, inside and outside!

Now, I appreciate this all sounds very 'Disney,' and very imaginative, very magical. That's fine! Your mind, and, in particular, your subconscious mind, is, in itself, a programme. 'What you think about you bring about.' Have you heard that saying? Many of the spiritual masters and teachers tell us that, and so do Psychologists and Psychiatrists. Your thoughts programme your behaviour and to change that, visualisation and imagination are key tools for transformation. What you imagine, you create, just like that! You are sending a new programme into your subconscious by doing this, and this, in turn, sends a new programme into the body, the actions and the behaviours. Your behaviours are determined by the programme of your thoughts and beliefs. If you believe, deep down (as I clearly did), that your inner child is dirty, shameful and disgusting, then your behaviour will automatically reflect that.

You will never feel good enough, clean enough, worthy enough or happy enough until this is changed, cleared, cleaned and released. By doing so, you are creating a new programme of worth, and so much more.

Exercise 2 - Letting go of anger.

Another 'essential' part of healing you, is to release the anger, rage and hate that is locked inside you. That anger isn't all against you – some of it is, but a lot of it is against your abuser. It may also be against your parents, siblings and other family for not noticing, not rescuing, not caring. It needs to come out, for as long as it stays inside you, it is you that hurts. Let's get it out now.

Go back to the garden. This is now your safe place, your sacred place. It is the place where you can be you, be safe, be accepted, be free. (If your abuse took place in a garden though, you may want to choose a different place. It doesn't matter where, as long as you feel safe.)

Bring back in Mini-Me and give them big cuddles.

We are going to allow, encourage and support Mini-Me to vent, release, punish, hurt or do anything they want to do to their abuser, without limitation or judgement, and to those who let them down. Remember, children and teenagers who are angry want to lash out. Some want to kill their abuser.

Now I know this sounds all very violent and 'not nice,' and this may not feel right for you, but this isn't about you. You are the grown up, and probably, a quite sensible, non-violent person. However, is your Mini-Me non-violent? I know my Mini-Me wasn't! She wanted to pummel and punish her abuser and make him suffer the way he'd made her suffer! The teen me wanted to 'stab the bastard,' and the young adult me wanted to castrate him. See? So, we are going to allow them to do this. Vengeance and revenge are normal, healthy reactions and responses. If we allow this revenge within the safety of our imagination, it is as powerful as if it were in real life, in terms of releasing and getting it out, and a whole lot safer.

Create a safe way for Mini-Me to be able to express ALL of their rage. Use your imagination, create it. You can do this! Here are some ideas...

You could use a cage, like an animal cage (like in a zoo) and have the abuser in the cage. (It's important that Mini-Me feels safe.) Give Mini-Me stones to throw at him, or a water cannon, or a big gun, or whatever it is that they want.

If Mini-Me is scared, give them a protective outfit. This may be a suit of armour, a shield and sword. It may be a magician and a wand. It may be a dragon to burn the abuser up! Allow Mini-Me to create the punishment they, not you, wants to inflict, with whatever back-up they invent.

With family who didn't protect, you might create a court type scene, where Mini-Me can accuse and blame, shout and rant, or use the cage, or anything else that enables him/her to get it all out. Their frustration, disappointment, hurt, anger, rage, and the rest. Let it all come up and out.

Afterwards, when it's all out, take Mini-Me to the lake. I want you to imagine that this lake is magical healing water. It's warm, soothing and gentle. It has the ability to wash away pain, sorrow, hurt, etc., and to restore, balance, make safe and bring back to peace the light in the child. Hold them as you bathe them, purify them, restore them and heal them.

Well done. You've just gone a long way with *Moving Past the Past.*

These two exercises may need repeating several times until all of the anger and hate is out, until Mini-Me feels safe and heard, no longer invisible and no longer at risk. You will know when it's done.

Chapter 3 - Sexual Behaviour

So, what about sex? How does CSA change us sexually? Who are we really, under the abuse? We don't know, because sexually, we don't know anything else other than who we are right now. It's truly wonderful when you find the real you, after you start to heal. This is the real 'sexual you,' the 'you' that you would have been, had the abuse not happened.

I've heard male clients ask me, "Am I gay?" because a man abused them and they responded sexually. No, you aren't gay.

"Am I a slut?" some female clients have asked, because they became promiscuous. No, you aren't a slut.

"Am I frigid?" asks another, because they feel nothing sexually. Also another no.

"Am I sick, twisted, weird?" because they fantasise about domination or submission, or have other desires that are termed as 'fetishes.' Also no.

"What about porn?" another asked, because they are addicted to it, enjoy it, and feel that they shouldn't. Again, the answer is no.

So, let's unpick these. Having a sexual response whilst being abused does not mean that you want it nor does it mean that you like it. It certainly doesn't mean that you are gay, if it was same sex. It means that the body is responding automatically. Children as young as two years old will become aroused. Sexual responses of the body are natural, instinctive, and above all, they are biological. They are not the same thing *at all* as sexual responses within the energy, the emotions, or the mind. If you got 'turned on,' or aroused whilst being abused, it does not mean that you fancied, were attracted to, or desired this person. Any sexual response is natural, biological and is not your fault.

Being promiscuous and having many sexual partners does not mean that you are a slut. It means that your sexual boundaries are not in place. This is not your fault. Sexual boundaries are normally created naturally, organically and over many years. From pre-pubescent times, you will see and hear about attraction and about sex. You will be taught, through subtle and not so subtle language, body language, disapproval, approval, and many other factors, what is acceptable and what is not acceptable. For example, I heard in my social and family environment, that it was not okay to have sex before you were sixteen, that you should be 'in love' with the person, that you didn't have to necessarily be married to them, but that you did need to be in a committed relationship with them, and you had to be old enough.

At school, within my peers, 'giving top' (allowing your boyfriend to touch your breasts), and 'giving bottom' (allowing him to touch you 'down there'), were milestones in relation to your age and relationship. At thirteen or fourteen it seemed that it was okay and acceptable to 'give top,' but not 'bottom.' Another year, and it had progressed to now being okay to 'give bottom' and by the following year it was okay to 'go all the way' (i.e. to have full, penetrative sex). These kinds of permissions are part of the society that we live in, and change depending on country, culture, tradition, parenting style, religion and many other restrictions. This is part of social norming, social culture and sexual and personal identity. However, when you have been exposed to sex and sexual behaviour too soon, too fast, too young - when those normal sexual boundaries have not had a chance to form and develop, they are simply not there. They do not exist. Add to this the fact that your body has been used, and may have been repeatedly used as a tool for someone else's sexual gratification, and it becomes a 'thing.' *Your body becomes a thing.* It's not important, not special, and not valuable; it's just a 'thing.' Add to that, the 'no sexual boundaries,' plus the 'body is a thing,' and then add on top of this, low or no self-esteem, feeling invisible, and the drive for love and affection. Now, add to all of that, the training that we have had from our abuser, that sex equals love and affection, and you have a hugely destructive mix. Can you see? It is not your fault!

The majority of CSA survivors repeatedly seek love through sex, rather than sex through love. They are addicted to the desire for affection and will repeatedly seek out partner after partner in their drive to fill the empty hole inside them. They will have sex with almost anyone who will show them attention. The rejection usually comes soon after, along with the sense of being used, both of which reinforce the belief that they are worthless, their body is worthless, and the esteem falls even further. It's time to repair it, the esteem, and to put in place sexual boundaries.

Liking, watching or being addicted to porn also falls within the area of sexual boundaries, as do fetishes and other 'unusual' sexual desires and drives. This too, is not your fault. There is no 'right' or 'wrong,' sexual behaviours to many CSA survivors. There is no acceptable or unacceptable 'sexual behavioural key' to turn on or off within their value system - they do not exist. The key is broken. The values are smashed. Mostly, they were never developed in the first place. They need to be repaired, fixed and put back in place. It's time to do that now. This is why you are here, reading this book. You want to repair.

Many people go completely the opposite by closing down sexually, totally and completely. Being 'frigid' does not mean you don't like or want sex; it means you are afraid of it, have shut down your sexual energy and desires and closed them off as a defence mechanism. <u>This is not your fault.</u> Your subconscious has created a belief that sex is dangerous, that sexual desire is sick, and your body has responded accordingly. Not surprising really. However, this belief no longer serves you, supports you or helps you. It prevents you from knowing the joy of sex and sexual contact with the right person.

Let us look at domination and submission now.

"How can anyone who has been abused like submission?" you may ask. Simple – it's about control. Yes, they are being dominated, but this time, they have some, or all, of the control. They are choosing this as a sex game, and that choice is powerful. It is the same with being the dominator – they finally have control. It gives back a sense of power; power that was stripped away at such a young age. Both domination and submission are forms of trying to take back power and control. Making sex a game, in some psychological way, makes it safer. Games are safe, games are fun, so turning sex into a game makes it easier and more enjoyable. And, because sex was never love, we don't see that keeping sex in a game prevents us from feeling real love from sex.

So, what should sex be? It should be, 'making love.' We have all heard the term, but don't really understand it. Let's try to now.

Love is energy. It flows, you can 'feel' it. Sex is energy, you can 'feel' that too, and when you love someone, you want to be close to them. Being in someone's arms, feeling their arms around you creates a bond, a closeness, and it's wonderful. As we kiss, arousal begins and the love feels strong. It flows up to the surface, and along with it, sexual energy begins to flow. The desire of this loving energy is to increase the closeness, and we move closer and closer 'into' that person, until we are literally 'inside' each other. We are climbing into their energy, and they are climbing into ours. As this happens, the love between us increases. We are literally 'making' love. We are making more love, we are increasing the love by adding to the love we already have. This is why it is called 'making' love.

Now, compare that to how it feels when we are having sex as 'sex games,' or having sex when we don't want to, when we feel obliged to – very different isn't it? Compare that to porn – that's just the body, that's just sexual energy flowing, there is no 'love' involved with this. There is no emotional closeness, there is no intimacy. There is just the flow of sexual drive and sexual energy. Love and closeness are totally absent. It is just a sex act. 'Act' is the appropriate word to use here, because we are 'acting.' We are not 'feeling.' You can't 'act' love. Do you see?

So, what we want to learn to do is to make love, and once we have, the difference is amazing. We have found something new, with depth, with joy, with feeling, and, after a while, we start to see the porn, the sex games, the other stuff, as shallow, empty, and meaningless, and we move further away from it. We are reprogramming our desires away from 'just sex' and onto love, and making love.

To do this, we need an open heart, to love our self, and to see ourselves as worthy, honourable, deserving, and we need to feel safe sexually. We also need to be with the right partner, one who we do truly love, and not just need. We also need to see our body as valuable, special and a gift; a gift to give and share, not a tool to take and be used. We will be doing an exercise shortly to begin this reprogramming and repair.

So, we have looked at all of these different sexual behaviours, and we can see that these have all developed from the childhood abuse. So, how do we change them? How do we build these new values, these new boundaries? How do we make a new key for our 'acceptable and unacceptable' limits and desires? How do we move our body from being a 'thing,' to being something very valuable?

It begins with self-love and self-esteem. Sounds simple but it's not. For a start, we don't love our self. Mostly we don't even like our self! And, for some, we actively hate our self. We certainly don't respect our self – we don't know what that is! And, we don't respect our body. Remember, it's just a 'thing.' For us to find our sexual boundaries, we have to learn all of these things – love, respect, value for ourselves, and value for our body. Now, the good news is, that we actually do know all these things.

"Aye?" I hear you say. "She just said that we don't know how! Now she's saying we do. What?"

Yes, you do know. You know how to love *others*. You know how to respect *others*. You know how to give to *others*, to be kind to *others*. But, you have no clue how to give any of this to you, because you never have. After all, you hated you, and who wants to do nice things for someone we hate? Who wants to value and appreciate someone we despise? We don't! They aren't worth it. You also need to be honest with you, open with you, accepting of you, and you have to start with being kind, to you!

KIND: I love that word. I also love the word HONOUR. They both say everything we need. Think about it for a moment. How many times a day do you criticise yourself, beat yourself up, and put yourself down? Loads I expect. Do you honour you? No. But you do honour others. You listen, you care, you stand up for, you protect, you support, you understand, you care - for *others*. Now, all you have to do is turn it all around, so that all of those lovely things are facing you, going into you! Start now. Start today.

From this moment forward, you are your own new, best friend. You are making friends, with you. You are falling in love, with you!

How and why do we develop friendships and relationships? We see something in the other person that we like. We like their smile, their laugh, their humour, their honesty, their stories, their attitudes, their values. And, we want to spend time with them because we enjoy their company. Gradually, the friendship grows, and along with it, trust, closeness, and a bond. We value them, they are important to us. We respect them, and we treat them well.

Now, ask yourself, "If I criticised my friend day and night, always put them down, and always told them off, would that person be my friend for long? If I spent all our time together complaining and moaning, would they still be my friend?" No, I don't expect they would. No one wants to be around someone like that. It's hard work and it's depressing! So, be your own best friend, and treat *you* the way that you would treat them. Every time you open your mouth, ask yourself,

"Would I say this to my best friend?"

If it's a 'no,' then don't say it to you. If it's too late, and it's already popped out of your mouth, as soon as you realise it's a put down, apologise. Immediately! Say sorry to you. You would to your best friend!

You are learning to love yourself. You are learning to respect yourself. The more you do this, the more natural it is; the easier it is. Once you truly love and respect you and your body, your boundaries will come in, all by themselves. Things that are not right for you will feel 'not right.' They will feel uncomfortable, not at ease, not pleasurable. Again, ask yourself,

"Would I put my best friend through this?" or, "Would I think it's fair for my best friend to do this?" If it's a 'no,' don't put yourself through it!

Many of my clients are in long term relationships, and many allow sexual behaviour from their partner that they don't particularly want, because they think that they should. Umm, no! If you don't want sex, say no. If you're not in the mood, say no. If your partner pressures you for sex, tell them to back off. You are not honouring you and you are not respecting you. If you don't respect you, neither will they. Every time you say 'yes' when inner you is saying 'no,' you are ignoring yourself in just the same way that 'little you' was ignored. You are allowing abuse and you are turning a blind eye. And, if you are defending this behaviour right now, if you are arguing in your head as you read this, stop. What part of being pressured into sex is not abuse? What, it's not abuse because it's your partner? Wrong! It is. Don't get me wrong, your partner won't see it that way. After all, you've let them do what they want for years. It is not their fault that they walk all over you sexually. *You* are the one that has not set any boundaries. *You* are the one that ignores you and puts your needs to one side. *You* have not insisted on your right to say no, because you didn't know that you could. *You* have not insisted on your right to be respected, or to be valued, or to have a say. *You* are 'shushing' the inner you, you are turning a blind eye. Can you see? And can you see how easy it is to make that change?

Now, don't beat yourself up about this. I can feel the guilt pouring out of you right now for the way that you have been treating you. Don't! It's another one of those things that was *not your fault*. You didn't know any other way, but you do now. Remember earlier I said it was about taking responsibility? That is what you are doing, right now. You are forgiving yourself for past behaviour, and you are making a commitment to yourself to change that behaviour, right now. Remember, 'little you' was trained to accept sexual behaviour without question, without argument. This is a kind of programming, a brainwashing. We will be unpicking this one later, when we look at reprogramming the beliefs, but I want you to realise right now that you are on an *automatic behaviour of immediate acceptance to adhere to another's desires*. This means that you have been trained to 'do as you are told' sexually. Tell yourself that you no long need to do that, and start asking yourself, "Do I want sex right now?" when your partner asks for, or expects, sex.

Begin to ask and to listen to you.

Start protecting you, including your body. Start standing up for you. *This* is self-love. This is exactly what it is. It is putting your needs at the front of the queue instead of at the back. This is you listening to you.

Tell your partner, 'not tonight' when you're not in the mood, and stick to it. Yes, they will moan, they may sulk. Let them. It's only because they are not used to hearing 'no.' It's only because they don't know your boundaries - because they are new. They will get used to them. And if they don't, they can go. Yes, that is quite hard, isn't it?

Give them time to adjust to these new boundaries. Try to help them understand, and, go gentle on them, as it's not their fault. All the rules are suddenly changing around them about 'what's okay' and 'what's not okay,' and they are bound to be confused, but, if they truly love you, they will get their head around it. It may take a while though, so be prepared to 'tough it out' and don't give in. Give them a copy of this book and ask them to read it. This is why I wrote it, not just for you, but for your partners, so that they can understand you, and so that they can understand the new rules, the new behaviours, and, the new expectations.

For one client who started this new behaviour, her partner sulked for nearly a month, withdrew all affection, barely spoke to her and was really hard to be around. Just when she was ready to give up, he suddenly just accepted the new way, and peace resumed. As a result of this, some months later, she has a better, healthier, happier marriage now than she has ever had. It is based on a new respect, a deeper love and a stronger equality.

It is your responsibility to you and to your healing to begin this new way of being with yourself and with others, and to implement new actions to support you. This is putting self-love into practice, not just thinking it, not just talking about it – doing it.

Again, it will help you to ask yourself, "Would I expect my best friend to have sex if she didn't want to? Would I expect her to 'put up and shut up'?"

Can you feel that? Can you feel the difference in the energy as soon as it is someone else that we are talking about? The response is immediate, it is strong, and it is a loud 'NO.' Followed by a strong defensive, protective surge of energy towards her, and an indignation and annoyance or anger towards the partner that is bullying her into sex. And yet, when it is your partner, the response is different isn't it?

"Oh, he doesn't really pressure me, he's not like that."

Are we in denial here? We are good at denial, remember?

Every time you feel that denial, just check in with yourself. Is it denial or is it real? Do this by simply using the, 'if this was my best friend' trick. Your response will let you know which is which.

Now, let's do another exercise to get this self-love started. I have an audio download of this on my website if it will help you. -

<u>Learning to love yourself</u>

Exercise 3 – Learning to Love yourself

We are going to go into the body and imagine your heart - your 'emotional heart.' Your heart is your centre of, and for, love. Love for others and love for yourself. The aim is to open your heart fully to its own love, and to share that love with your body and with you.

Go back to the garden. Take as long as you need, and get yourself comfy. Settle yourself down in a safe, comfortable place and bring your attention into your heart. I want you to picture your heart as a flower. Now, imagine that this flower is behind a protective wall. This is your 'heart wall.' You created this wall to protect your heart when you were little.

Your heart desires to love, to be open, to be free, to have all the light shining into it, and to shine its light out, but this wall is blocking it. Your flower can't grow, it can't shine, and it can't share its love. This wall was created by you, made by you to protect this beautiful, gentle, loving heart from the nasty stuff that was going on at the time. It's been locked behind there ever since.

What is your wall made of? Stone, brick, metal, wood? Or, is it something else? How high is it? How thick are the walls? Have a walk around this wall. Is there any way in? Imagine going over the wall and having a look at your heart. What does it look like? Is it dark, battered and fragile? It needs light, and it wants the light. It wants to have no restrictions and no shade.

Now, find a way to remove the wall. Use your imagination. If it's made of wood, burn it. If it's stone or brick, imagine a big demolition machine, with one of those swingy balls on it, and smash the wall down. If it won't all come down, and all you can see is a hammer and chisel, work away at it a brick at a time, a stone at a time. It is essential that this wall comes down, all the way down! (This may take several sessions/attempts to get it all down.)

You may find that Mini-Me pops in and wants to help. After all, it's their wall! They built it! But, they don't need it now; they have you! You will protect them, you will keep them safe, and they can finally let their wall go.

Keep reassuring yourself (and little you if he/she is there) that you don't need this wall anymore, that you are safe now; that it is time for your heart to come out and shine.

Once the wall is down, imagine the sun pouring onto the flower, and it opening gently up. See it being restored, growing, and right in its centre, right in its nucleus, see the light beginning to shine out of it like a beacon, like a lighthouse. This light is your love! Let it shine.

It may be weak and watery – that's okay. It will get stronger and brighter very quickly once the wall has gone.

Now, imagine directing the light from that beam all around the chest, then up into the head, and down into the belly. Keep letting the light shine into the body, into every single bit, from the top of your head to the tips of your toes.

Next is to use this light to heal your body.

Look down into your sexual area. Do you see any restrictions, any barriers? Maybe something like a chastity belt, restricting you from sex? Maybe you see a load of darkness in your womb (if you are female) or around your penis and anus for men. Have a look – ask your body to show you. Then simply, pour the light of your love into it and see it, focus on it, visualise it all melting away.

Keep the intention of 'I am healing, I am letting go, I am ready, and I am safe.' Your thoughts are so very powerful, and it is with these powerful thoughts, and the powerful love that you have, that you will heal.

Once you have done as much as you can, take a moment to just simply bask in the light of this love; your love. It is as pure now as it was when you were an innocent babe. It was never tainted, it is still innocent, and it is beautiful.

You may feel quite emotional with this heart work. That's okay, just let it flow. When you are ready, come back from the garden and open your eyes.

Do this exercise repeatedly until your heart and love have developed as big as they will get. Keep healing your sexual areas until they, too, are well, at peace and happy.

Chapter 4 - The Emotional Body

Imagine a train. It has many, many carriages. This train is so long that it won't fit alongside the platform of any station, so, if you want to get off it, you will need to be in the first carriage - but you're not, you're in the last carriage, way at the back. Now, let's imagine that there is a station that you want to get off at, called 'Peace.' You want to try to climb over the other carriages in front of you to get to the front so that you can disembark the train, but there is no way through. There is no door, no corridor, and no escape into the carriages in front, only out through your own carriage door. You see the train approaching the 'Peace Station,' and it stops, but you can't get off the train – you are nowhere near the platform! And, before you know what's going on, the train is pulling out of the station, with you still on it, and you've missed your stop. 'Alright,' you think, 'I will get off at the next station!' But you can't, because the carriage that you are in won't fit on the platform of any station, so you're stuck on the train - a train called 'Chaos.' Every now and then, a new carriage is fitted to the 'Chaos Train,' and again, it's in front of your carriage. The station looks more and more out of reach. It is!

These other carriages, the ones in the way, they contain our baggage. It's all ours, every single carriage load, it's all ours! Why isn't it behind us? After all, our baggage was created in the past, so what's it doing up there, ahead of us, in the future, blocking our way, instead of behind us, in the past?

It is there because we drag our baggage with us everywhere we go; into every situation, into everything. It keeps growing, because with every passing hurt, failed relationship, broken friendship, with every turn, we add more baggage. And it's in the way. It's blocking us, our life and our way forward. And it keeps growing! If we have used relationships to heal, but they ended up broken, another carriage of baggage is added. If we turn to drink, drugs, gambling, etc., we add another carriage.

So, how do we get off this train? Well, this 'train' is 'life.' It is the train of life, of living, of existing. We have to be on 'A' train, but we don't have to be on 'this' train! If we can unpack, unload or uncouple those other carriages carrying all of all our baggage, we can get off the 'Chaos Train' at the 'Peace Station' at last, and there, we will find a new train. A much nicer one!

I know you want that. I did too. I've been on my 'Peace Train' for some years now, and it's lovely! I'd like to share my train with you. In fact, I already am because you're reading this book, which means you are now part of my life, my journey, and I am part of yours. Nice isn't it? Don't get me wrong, I've messed up a few times since being on the 'Peace Train.' I always know when I have because 'Peace' is missing. I've accidentally stepped off it and onto the wrong train, going the wrong way. As soon as I realised, I uncoupled my latest baggage, and stepped back onto the 'Peace Train' as quickly as I could.

So, how do you uncouple these unwanted carriages of baggage? How do we get rid of the baggage? We empty them, carriage by carriage. What is our baggage? It's our emotions mainly. It's also our thoughts and beliefs, our programming, but we will come onto those in the next Chapter. Let's focus, for now, on emotions.

Feelings! They are so very powerful and so very natural. We are emotive, responsive, reactive beings you know. If you want to know who we are naturally, spend half an hour watching a toddler. Within a space of thirty minutes, they will probably go through at least a dozen different emotions - from rage, to tears, to laughter and back again, all in an instant. Notice the way each one came and went so quickly? One at a time – created, felt, expressed – next! Notice the way there is no grudge building? They don't hang on to anything, it all just moves through them and then it's forgotten, it's gone. For a toddler, emotions are automatic. They have no filter, no pre-programming of what is acceptable and what is not. That, they learn later. Over the next five to ten years, we are taught what and which emotion is acceptable and what and which is unacceptable. We are also taught what is an acceptable volume, length and speed of these feelings, and we suck it all up like a little sponge. Let me explain.

Have you heard this one? 'You should be over that by now.'

Or, have you heard this one? "Big girls don't cry. Boys don't cry unless they're a sissy. You're weak, be strong; strong is good - strong is better!" (Ergo, don't show any emotion, be a robot!). "Anger is nasty, nasty people aren't liked, no one likes a temper, it's a tantrum, you are a bad girl/boy," because you are displaying anger. (Ergo, anger makes you a bad person; no one likes a bad person, so no one will like you.)

As humans, we have a natural drive to people please, to be part of, and to be accepted. We are social creatures and the worst punishment for us is isolation. We will do almost anything to stay within the social group and be accepted, so, we conform.

Here are some more. "Don't argue, don't answer back, I'll give you something to cry about! You deserve to be punished. I'm going to give you a hiding." And bang, the hiding comes, and we are not allowed to display fear, because that's weak, and we are not allowed to display anger, because that makes us bad, and we are being punished because we deserve it, and that too, makes us bad. And on and on these programmes go.

And that is what they are you know, programmes. By the time we are about eight years old, we have learned to suppress, repress, push down, ignore, reject, avoid and distract ourselves from all of our negative feelings. I say negative feelings, because on the whole, most of us were 'allowed' to be happy, cheerful, to sing, to laugh, to giggle. We were being taught/programmed that positive emotions are good, and allowed, permitted, acceptable, and that negative feelings were bad, unacceptable and not permitted.

So, what's it like for the emotion? Emotions are energy. Think of the word 'emotion' and focus on the first letter of 'e.' 'E' stands for energy. What is left of the word now, without the 'e'? 'Motion.' So, emotion is simply 'energy in motion.' Energy is designed to flow, to move, and to be expressed. We are humans, not robots, and we are feeling beings. All emotions are a natural response to a given situation. Let me say that again, 'All emotions are a natural response to a given situation.' Whether they are positive or negative is irrelevant, they are the appropriate emotional response in that moment and they are there to teach us, to show us, to help us, whether they are positive or negative.

When I encounter a situation or event where a feeling of 'happiness' is generated, I feel happy. The emotional response of 'happiness' is showing me that I like the thing that I just did that generated the feeling of happiness; I want more of it, I want to do it again. Likewise, the same thing happens with the negative emotions. When I feel a negative emotion I want to withdraw, back off from and stay away from the thing that caused me that feeling.

Let's start dismantling some of these so-called negative emotions for a moment.

Let's take anger. When we feel anger in response to a situation, the anger is showing us something. It is usually a response to a situation where someone or something has overstepped the mark, crossed the line, disrespected us or taken us for granted. The emotional response called 'Anger' is teaching us that the event, the action or the behaviour was not okay, not acceptable, and we should move away from it, or confront it. The main thing is that we didn't like it. Good! We shouldn't like it! Now that we have felt the anger, and figured out that something that just happened was not okay, the next step is, "So, what do you want to do about it?" The anger has done its job. It has showed us a line, a boundary that has been crossed, and we have just realised this, so anger can now go. The next bit, the response, is up to us. We can choose to let the bad behaviour that caused the anger go, or we can choose to confront it or correct it. If anger had not surfaced, we may not have realised or understood that someone had just mistreated us, and then it may happen again. The anger is helping us, it is our friend, our ally. So, let's start seeing these emotions as helpers, all of them, the positive and the negative ones.

If I feel fear, that emotion is telling me I am at risk, I am in danger and I need to get away and get safe. It is trying to protect me, to help me. When I feel grief and loss because someone I love has gone away or died, that is the normal, appropriate response. It is showing me that I am sad, that I will miss that person, and that I valued them. It is showing me that I loved them. Emotions are all valid and they are all good. There are no 'bad' emotions. Allow that to sink in for a moment, because we are going to go and 'talk' to all of the emotions that are locked inside you shortly and you need to be friends with them and understand them, or they won't talk to you!

Now, one of these emotions is a little bit more complicated. It's called 'Guilt.' Guilt is generated as a natural response when we have done something wrong. It is trying to teach us values, to be decent people. Guilt feels horrible, and we don't like feeling horrible, and this teaches us that the thing that we just did, this action we did, or those words that we just spoke, were not okay. It may have been that we hurt someone or something, or we let someone down, we broke a promise, or said hurtful words, and now we feel guilt. "Okay guilt, thanks, lesson learned. I didn't like the feeling that was generated out of that action; I won't be doing that again in a hurry." Guilt is teaching us right from wrong - internal value building. After that feeling of guilt comes, we will make efforts to try not to deliberately hurt another so that we don't have to feel that awful guilt response again. Make sense?

I want you to begin to see emotions as our internal teachers. They are not our enemy, they are our teachers. Got it? Good stuff, because it's so important to understand our emotions and accept them, and we can't do that when we deny them, ignore them or suppress them.

Now, when I say 'guilt is a complicated one,' I say this because we can often feel the emotion of guilt when we haven't done anything wrong. Someone can 'put a guilt trip on us' because in their eyes, we have done something wrong. But it's not their eyes that matter, it's ours! The emotion called 'Guilt' means that I have messed up, I have made a mistake. That's okay, I am allowed to make mistakes - it's how we learn. Now, when someone tells us we are bad, we immediately feel guilt, even if we haven't done anything wrong. The need to please others and be liked is strong in us, and when we can see that someone is displeased with us, we immediately feel that we have done something wrong, or they wouldn't be displeased with us, so guilt is generated as a response. What we need to do, is to examine it, have a chat with it, the guilt.

"Have I done anything wrong here, or not?" you ask yourself, and you examine your actions, attitudes, words and behaviour. If the answer is 'not,' then it's okay to **let Guilt go**. If the answer is "Yes, I have messed up," then thank Guilt for showing you that, do your best to put it right, make amends, and take the learning not to do it again, and **let Guilt go.**

All of these emotions were meant to be a teaching tool, to show you something, and then they are meant to go on their merry way, having done their job. That is how it should be. But, we have already discussed programming and the way we are taught to judge our emotions as either being okay or not okay, acceptable or not acceptable, and we have been taught to push down and suppress all the negative ones. So, let's now imagine where they go, these emotions that we have suppressed.

Emotions were designed and created in our belly, (that's where we generate the energy of emotions), and, as they are released, they come up. They move up through our chest, up our throat and then out through our mouth or eyes. (It's like a dragon breathing out smoke or fire.) Again, to remember how it's meant to be, watch a toddler. The very strong ones will pulse throughout the whole body and make you shake as they come out, such as anger and rage, terror and panic, but out they are meant to come and need to come. They were not designed to be locked in a cell, trapped for eternity, inside us. They try to come out; they rattle the cage, shake the box and try to escape, but we just keep pushing them back in and telling them to, "Shush." This goes on for a long time, until the box, the cell, the cage, the ball, whatever your emotions have been shoved into, starts to explode, or leak. Sometimes it releases in little puffs like a volcano, and then calms down again. I call these volcano ones, 'panic attacks.' I call the leaking gently out ones, 'depression.' I call the explosive ones a 'psychotic break.' (These are not medical terms, they are the way I see them and the way I work with them.) They don't all come out, just enough to ease the pressure in the ball for a while, and to create some room for some new ones.

Our ball (as I will now call it), is meant to be there. Whilst emotions were designed to be created, felt and released, there is also an internal safety mechanism to delay them when we are at extreme risk. I call this mechanism 'the ball.' Let me explain. We haven't changed biologically in 50,000 years. Let's imagine we are in a tribe, and next door's tribe has come over and slaughtered all our family, or a tiger has come and killed my family and is now trying to get me, I am not safe. My priority, my survival instinct, is to get safe first. Now, I am going to be feeling a whole raft of different emotions from watching this slaughter – grief, shock, loss, rage, fear and more, but if I start feeling them now, I am going to get slaughtered too! I haven't got time to cry, to rant, to be upset – I have to get safe. So, all those emotions go and park themselves in the ball, so that I can't feel them right now, enabling me to focus on my own safety and survival. My adrenalin is surging into fight, flight or freeze, and I choose 'flight,' and I run. Now, imagine it's a few hours later, I am now safe, I have stopped the heavy breathing, my adrenalin has calmed down a lot, my body has returned to normal, and now my ball can empty. I can now release all of those emotions from earlier. It's really important that I empty this ball as soon as possible, because those emotions are toxic, heavy and weigh me down. My body can also feel them, and my adrenal gland can't calm down properly because it can still feel the fear in my body, locked inside. My body is still hearing and feeling fear even though the danger has passed. My body can still feel shock, even though the event has now passed. These emotions are giving messages into my body that go right up to my brain, and my subconscious mind – you are in danger, you are not safe, etc. I am now looking for the danger, even though it has gone, and I can't find it, so now I am confused, because every part of me says, "Danger, danger!" Do you see?

It has to come out, and now, because tomorrow there may be another tiger, another slaughter, and I need my ball to be ready to take in more, and I need my body to be strong. Or, tomorrow may be a lovely, joyful, happy day, but I won't be able to feel that good stuff because there is too much fear and shock still in me, blocking my joy, from this thing that happened today. If I don't get them out, I will constantly be feeling at risk, and I will spend my life feeling and thinking that I am not safe, even when I am, because the fear is still in there. They don't have a 'sell by date' you know, these emotions. They don't 'go off.' They will sit there until we let them out, and they will sit there for years, decades, and right up to our graves, if we let them. They will skew our perspective on life, on safety, on love, on everything. They will drive us, even though the event that created them has long since passed - they are still there, screaming, "Danger!" at the top of their lungs. Do you see?

It has to come out. We have to open the ball and let them out, and they want to come out, honestly they do. But, it's not easy. You will feel some of these 'feelings' as they move through you, and it's not nice. You will feel that old fear, that old disgust, that old shame. You will feel it all, but once it's out, it's out! Your body will begin to reset to peace, to safety, to tranquillity, to everything you want it to. It is hard work, getting this lot out, but I promise you, it's worth it.

Now, let's talk about how these emotions drive us.

Control freak? That means you don't feel safe inside, and taking control is the only way that you can feel safe. Once the fear is out, you will be less controlling because you will know that you are safe anyway, control or not.

Jealous? This just means that you are deeply insecure, with very strong feelings of inadequacy. There is a belief in you that says you are not good enough. This means that there are emotions of unworthy, undeserving and inadequate inside your ball. These will drive you, your behaviour and your actions. It is because you feel so unworthy, so unlovable, so 'not good enough,' that you see everyone as a threat. The automatic thought is that your man/woman will like that person more than you, because deep down inside, you feel unworthy. Once that 'unworthy' is out, you will be able to build up self-belief and self-confidence, to know that you are the wonderful person that you are, and begin to realise that your partner is with you because they love you and because you are worthy. The fear of losing him/her to another will go, and in its place will be a new feeling – a sense of security within the relationship. Your trust begins to build. You are trusting that you are good enough, you are worthy, and as a result, your jealousy and mistrust goes. (That is, of course, unless there is something to really be mistrustful of, in which case, let him/her go, because you deserve more!)

Self-blame, disgust, shame – yep, they are going to be there. Children blame themselves for most things. Parents' divorce –

'must be my fault - if I was nicer, better, they would have been happier and wouldn't have split up.' Strange the way the child's mind works, isn't it? It is highly likely that your Mini-Me thinks that the abuse was their fault, that in some way, they were to blame. NOT TRUE. And you need to get that out!

This emotional work is probably the hardest part of our train journey, because we fear our fear. Don't. You are safe now. It's important to relax as much as you can when you are doing any emotional work. As your body releases its pain and shame, it will tense and it will be drained. The more you can relax, the quicker your body will reset and restore. I meditate every day, and find it essential for my wellbeing. There are many ways to help you relax and many meditation and relaxation CDs, audios and downloads out there. Find something that works for you. I have several of my own in my shop on my website, but it doesn't have to be mine. We will talk more about this in the Support Chapter later in the book.

The Energy Field

Before we get onto releasing our emotions, I need to explain a little more about energy. We have discussed the energy of emotions, and that is easy to understand because we can feel them. But there is more energy that you are probably not aware of – and that is our own energy field. Some call it an aura or an auric field.

Science calls it a magnetic field. It doesn't matter what you call it, but it is there. It is invisible to the naked eye, and it surrounds us. Our energy field is usually around three to five feet wide, front, back and sides (or one to two metres), and about two feet above us and below us (one metre). We are magnetic beings, with magnetic resonance and the energy field can get out of balance and be very negative. In people suffering with depression, for example, it is filled with the negative emotions of helplessness, hopelessness, despair and fear. You may have heard the expression, 'It's like I'm walking around with a big, black cloud all around me.' Yes, quite true, that is exactly what it is. If you had a big, black cloud around you all the time, would you be able to see the sun, feel its warmth and know happiness? I wouldn't! You would also feel tired a lot and everything would be a huge effort. This is because negative energy is dark and heavy, whilst positive energy is light and bright. It's important you realise just how damaging negative energy is. It saps our life, our light, our joy and our peace. We see life through a fog of fear, a mist of pain, darkness and despair. Imagine carrying this around with you every day, year on year. Now, imagine how heavy that ball is in your tummy! With its weight, its toxicity, leaking into us day in day out, is it any wonder many of us get gut issues, food intolerances, chronic fatigue? Imagine all those negative thoughts in the head there, and yes, they have energy too. How hard is it for the head to carry that? No wonder we get migraines and pressure headaches. So, when we do this emotion release work, we also need to clear and clean all this negative stuff from our energy field too.

So, now let's start releasing some of these emotions aye? Let's begin by making friends with them and with your ball.

Exercise 4 – Releasing the Emotions

Go back to the garden. Make your intention clear – you are here to empty your ball and clean your energy field.

Go to the lake and allow yourself to bathe in its tranquil, healing waters. Visualise your energy field around you, and allow it to clear and clean in the water. Imagine the water washing through it, drawing the negative energy away from you and into the lake. Feel your own energy getting lighter, brighter, almost as if someone just turned the sun up in the garden. The water may change colour as it does this, becoming dark and inky, but that's fine, it will soon clear. The lake will sterilise, neutralise and clean it all away.

Once this is done, you will feel stronger, calmer and more focused. Now, go into your heart. Open your heart up and shine the light of your love down and into your ball. This light is filled with love, compassion, patience, care and kindness. Imagine your ball. What colour is it? What is its shape, size, density? What is it made of? Is it hard like stone, or rubbery, or soft and squidgy?

Allow your ball to be however it looks to you. Talk to it, make friends with it, and then begin to talk to the contents of the ball. Each and every emotion has a name, has a reason to be there, and it won't come out if it's scared of you or if it's scared of your judgement or condemnation. One by one, name them and say hello.

"Hello 'Fear,' I am so sorry that you're scared. You're allowed to be scared, but it's okay now, 'cos the thing that made you scared has gone away now - you can stop hiding and come out." Imagine fear as a cloud, rising up from the ball, moving its way out of you. Allow it to go any way it wants to. This may be up and out through your breath, or out through your crown at the top of your head. It may come out through your belly button, or through your heart. As it comes out of you, it will gently dissolve, fade away, drift away and disappear into the peace of the garden.

Then, go onto the next one.

"Hello, Shame, I love you. There is no longer any reason to feel shame. You did nothing wrong and I am here for you. It's time to go now, Shame, go out and find your peace. Look how beautiful this garden is, go find your peace now, Shame." And see 'shame' gently go.

Keep working with the ball until each and every emotion has made its way out. You may cry, you may feel angry, you may feel fear. You may feel any of these emotions and more, as they make their way up and out of you, but don't panic and don't be scared.

Know and trust that they are exiting, that you are safe, and that the emotion you are feeling as it leaves your body will soon pass.

Once the ball has emptied, you will see that it has shrunk. Now, ask the healing energy of the lake to go into the ball and cleanse it and purify it inside. You might feel that you can pull the ball out and wash it in the lake, or that the energy of the water can simply find its way into you and into your ball. However you imagine it to be, is just right.

You will need several trips to the lake to empty your ball. Even after you empty it, when you go back next time, it may be full again for a while. The ball will act like a little vacuum bag, sucking up all the stuck and locked emotions from everywhere within your body. You will find there are a lot within your sexual areas. These will need to make their way up, or down to the ball, depending where they are in the body.

At another 'ball' session, ask Mini-Me to come in, and take him/her to the lake. Clear their emotional ball too. Call in as many versions of Mini-Me's as there are. They all carry emotions and they all need to empty them out.

What you are aiming for here is **emotional neutrality**. To be neutral is to feel totally indifferent to an event – you don't care one way or another, it simply doesn't matter, it's not important; it's just something that happened long ago. There is no reaction, nothing, anywhere in the body, the mind or the emotions. That's when it's neutral. If there are any feelings rising up when you think of an event, you are still attached to the event emotionally. This means the emotion that was created at the time of the event is still present, still there, still very much alive, and locked within you. We want the emotions to go, all of them. Yes, it will leave the event in its place, but without the emotion to go with it, it loses all its power. Does that make sense? I will give you an example: until I did this release work, I could not watch any television programme or film with any kind of sexual abuse or rape in it. None! It made me feel sick, shaky; awful! There was an immediate reaction of disgust, fear and horror. If I did catch something by accident, I would rush to turn it off, especially the sound. I would feel very upset inside, disturbed within my energy on multiple levels. I may have nightmares and bad dreams that night, and maybe for several nights until it settled back down. That reaction that came flying up is the emotional attachment to the event of my abuse. The programme or film has triggered a response, a reaction, and up it comes.

The work you are doing here, this emotional release work changes all of that. Those powerful reactions are no longer there, they have gone. If I think back to my abuse now, I feel nothing. Not upset, not angry, not sad; nothing! I am neutral to it. I am not upset and I am not happy. I am just indifferent. The result of this is freedom, choice, and empowerment. I am now free to watch what I want, when I want. This is new! One of my favourite television programmes of the last few years is 'Law and Order: SVU'[20] (Special Victims Unit). For those of you that don't know it (and I doubt you watch it), it is a programme about a New York police department that deals especially and only with rape and sexual abuse cases – the 'special victims.' I never miss an episode. Do you see the shift here? There is no way on earth that I would have either wanted to watch it, or have been able to watch it before I did the clearance and healing work on my emotions. This is the same work I am sharing with you here, in this book.

Now, once your emotional reactions are all gone, you may choose not to watch a programme like that, but this is the point – it will be your choice. When you are full of reactions, there is no choice – you simply can't. It's too painful. I want you to have that choice – don't you?

When you do this work, you need to obviously clear all the emotion from the abuse itself, but you will also need to clear all the hurt and chaos *since* your abuse too. I had many failed relationships to clear, including an abusive one, plus the grief of three miscarriages, hurt created from failed jobs and friendships, and my deep sense of failure on multiple levels. And then there is all the family stuff too, that's all got to go! It all needs to come out.

In so doing, you are emptying your carriages, you are uncoupling them. Your carriage, the one you are sitting on, which was at the back of the train, is now getting closer to the front.

It took me three weeks to empty my ball, and that was me working on it every single day, using all of my knowledge and all of my understanding, and it was the toughest thing I ever had to do. I cried buckets, I howled like a wounded animal, I shook with rage and anger, and then I cried some more. I 'cried me a river' as the song says, but at the end of my river was my rainbow. It just appeared, one day out of the blue, when I was in the lake and went into my ball, and I found that my ball was simply empty! And then the sun came out, at last!

Let this emotional release work take as long as it takes for you. Don't rush it, don't push it. This is hard, draining, exhausting work, getting this old stuff out, but it is so worth it, I promise you. And, it will never be this difficult again. In the future your ball will function and work well. It will be easy to clean, empty, restore and reset in a matter of minutes. Since I emptied my ball, I regularly check in with myself, my heart, and my ball. It fills back up quite quickly in times of stress you know, and needs to be emptied regularly, but it never takes long, and it's rarely very hard, because there isn't much in there. This is partly because I never let it get too full, and partly because I live a much more peaceful and settled life these days, so there is less to go in there in the first place.

Now, it's your turn. You can do this, you are strong enough and you are ready!

Chapter 5 - The Mental Body

The mind – a minefield! Now, don't panic but you need to understand the way your mind works if you are ever going to *Move Past the Past*, because it's got a huge amount to do with your behaviour and mental wellbeing. Let me help you to get to grips with it, because it is your most powerful tool and when you can get it to work for you, instead of against you, it can transform your life.

Do your thoughts destroy, or create? Help, or hinder? Get in the way or light the way?

Your mind is very much like a computer. It comes with a pre-programme installed, and with lots of disk space to add new data. It's just like buying a laptop; it's either a Windows or a Mac: no matter how much work you do, you cannot make a Mac into a Windows – it isn't! And, you can't uninstall the pre-programme - you can do a factory reset, but it will still be a Mac or a Windows. Got that bit so far? Excellent! The good news is, is that the pre-programme that is installed (the one that can't be deleted), is really positive and helpful. It is our centre of safety, happiness and confidence. To convince you of this ('cos I can feel your doubts here), just look at any two year old child. They have the self-confidence of God! They are naturally happy, loving and cuddly, and they are, above all, fearless! This is who we truly are, I promise you.

Oftentimes, people come to me and say, "I've lost my confidence," or, "I've lost my happiness." Nope, it's still there, locked in the pre-programme (it's the 'Mac' or the 'Windows' bit), it can't be deleted!

So, where is it then? Where's it gone? Why can't I feel it, find it, access it? Well, it's got buried under a tonne of other stuff – stuff that came later!

To find it, this original 'happy, safe' programme, we need to have a clear out of all the rubbish that's on top of it.

Let me explain.

Children's minds are like little sponges. There is no filter – they believe everything they are told. They also believe everything they hear and see. They learn by copying, watching and listening. The filter starts to come in at around the age of ten or eleven years of age. It gradually develops, and they start questioning, doubting, and forming their own beliefs over the next fifteen years or so. Until that point, everything they see, hear and absorb, forms a new programme - a new bit of data, and this data is added to the 'computer' (the brain, the subconscious mind,) as a new programme. This is a bit like adding a new word document to your computer – it's there, filed. When you need it, you go and find the file and use it. That is just how our mind works. Now, these files, these programmes, they form our beliefs, and our beliefs drive our actions, behaviours and attitudes.

Let's talk a little bit about our conscious and subconscious mind. We've all heard of them, and most of us have a basic understanding of how they work. We know that the subconscious is the underlying bit, the bit that is the 'sub,' under the surface, and we know that we do things subconsciously, automatically, but most people don't really understand how that works, so let me explain.

Your conscious mind is the bit at the top. It is your reasoning, thinking, rational mind; your intelligent mind, your control mind, your ego mind – it is the mind that is in charge, it is the Boss, or so it thinks! Nope - wrong. (If that were true, and you were trying to lose weight, you'd stay away from the cakes and chocolate!) Now, imagine underneath the conscious mind, down in the basement is an archive storage room. This room is filled with filing cabinets and these cabinets hold all of your thoughts and all of your beliefs, going back all time – right to when you were born. Clever stuff aye? This archive storage room is the 'subconscious mind,' the mind under the surface, and it's huge! Imagine how many thoughts and beliefs are in here! Every insult, every put down, every snipe or dig that ever upset you – they are filed in these drawers as beliefs. Whether they are true or not is irrelevant. At some point your mind absorbed these insults as a fact, and filed them. Think back for a moment just to a three year period, say thirteen to sixteen (the time when we are all hyper sensitive, unsure and hormonal). Spotty? Filed. Ugly? Filed. Fat? Thin? Filed. Not fast enough, not clever enough, not good enough? Filed. Dirty, disgusting, sick? Filed. Unsafe, at risk? Filed.

How would it be if I told you that it is thes   , these beliefs that drive your behaviour? Yep, it's got n   do with your conscious mind upstairs – the so-called Boss   everything to do with your subconscious mind downstairs. I   he thoughts and beliefs down here in the basement that drive   behaviour.

Feel insecure, unsure and fearful? Then you   ehaviour will reflect the beliefs held in those drawers that drive   at - the beliefs that say,

"I am not safe."

Now, these beliefs most certainly used to be true, but are they true now? Hopefully, they are not. Hopefully, you have a life now that is safe, but does your mind know that? Have you told it that? Do you say to yourself, "I am safe now?"

Probably, you have not. And, have you destroyed those old beliefs that say that you're not safe? Also probably not – because you didn't know they were there! Well, you do now!

The good news is that these cabinets also hold the original thoughts and beliefs - you know, the ones you were pre-programmed with - but they are right at the back of the cabinets, way behind a whole lot of other stuff, the stuff that says, "I am useless, rubbish, dirty, disgusting. I am unsafe, at risk, in danger."

It is these beliefs that drive this sabotaging, destructive behaviour. Let's have a look at that now – the reaction to the action of the thoughts.

Most of us can't abide lies and secrets. Of course not, because if our childhood had been open, transparent and honest, the abuse either wouldn't or couldn't have happened in the first place, and, if it did, it would have been stopped very quickly because it would have been expressed and verbalised and all come out in to the open. We are very aware of this, and so we tend to 'over react' to lies, dishonesty and untruths, and secrets cause us huge angst. There are no shades of grey to us – there is black and there is white. There are lies and there is truth. There is secrecy and there is transparency. However, most of the rest of the population are not quite so black and white in their view of the truth, nor in their view of secrets, and their shades of grey can cause immense problems for us.

So, what happens when we catch someone in a lie? Those lies create in us a reaction of fear – we immediately feel unsafe, at risk and threatened. This is because the 'new lie' is looking for a place to be filed, and it goes into the existing 'lies' cabinet, and when that cabinet is opened, a whole lot of old, nasty stuff with all the lies from our past comes springing up. We are reacting not only to the new lie, but to all of the old ones too. The new lie is 'triggering' all of the old lies in the cabinets – the ones that really did put us at risk, and our behaviour reacts accordingly. This behaviour is destructive and very powerful, and we have little or no control over it. We are often accused by our partners or children of 'over reacting,' or being a 'drama queen,' or of 'looking for a fight,' and more. It is true, we are over reacting, but we can't control it. We are over reacting to the current event, but if we add that current event to the old lies, we can begin to understand why the reaction was as powerful as it was.

The way to deal with this is to keep reassuring yourself that you are safe now, that you are an adult and that you are in control. Alongside this reassurance we need to clear out the old beliefs that tell us that lies are so terribly dangerous.

Control – when we have it, is paramount; it is another layover from the CSA. Clearly we had zero control during our abuse and bad things happened. As a defence mechanism, our mind decides that, had we had control, we would have been safe, so 'control' becomes a default mechanism for 'safe.' We feel the need to be in charge, to make decisions, to feel empowered, because deep down, we don't! Our partners and children will accuse us often of being control freaks, and they are right, but they don't understand why we are like this, or how to deal with it.

On top of this are the triggers of rejection and abandonment. If we feel someone doesn't really want us or want to spend time with us, we will often push them away before they push us away, and again, we act and react accordingly. This reaction is to save us from the pain of rejection, but often it just creates isolation and loneliness for us.

In addition to this, there is often the issue of affection – we can be too tactile and too clingy, or, just the opposite - too cold and too distant. We will often withdraw into our 'cave,' with, what seems to other people, little or no reason. Once in our cave, we are cold, distant, hostile and often aggressive if pushed. In fact, what we need most of the time is space to calm down from our inner reaction and we will come out of that withdrawal all by ourselves. But, at other times, we need to feel loved, reassured and coaxed out of our cave by our partner.

Another reaction we often see is the overprotective parent. Many of my clients watch their children like a hawk, and feel unable to give their child the normal freedom that other children have. The children of abused parents are often not allowed to participate in sleep overs, or go to friends' houses, or the park, or go on school trips without the parent accompanying them. The fear that something will happen to their children, as it did to them, controls and consumes them. It's not a great life for the child, and when they become teenagers, demanding freedom, there are huge issues for the abused parent in letting go. One of my clients insisted her teenager text or ring her every hour when he was out, to let her know he was safe and okay - and he was seventeen! He had no idea why his mum was 'so paranoid' but he adhered, most of the time. When he didn't, his mum had panic attacks so badly that she was very ill. The child lived in guilt and the parent lived in angst. Not a great way, for either of them!

Another trait that we often have is to constantly look for reassurance and validation. "Do I look nice?" or, "Is this okay?" We won't just ask once, we will repeat and ask again for the same validation. It can often drive our partner nuts!

All this behaviour can make us very hard to live with! So, how do we change it?

I use hypnosis. Hypnosis is a tool that has been used for thousands of years. It works by going into the subconscious and having a good sort out, a good clear out, a refiling session. We clear out all the beliefs that no longer serve you, the ones that are outdated, no longer true and we delete them. Just like a computer, if we don't want a file, we press delete. Just like a filing store, you can shred, burn, destroy and remove all of these old beliefs. And, while we are there, we can get the ones that were never true in the first place too. Thoughts that say, "I am a spotty, nerdy, insecure teenager?" Or the ones that say, "I have no control, no power, no voice." And the ones that say, "I am invisible, I don't matter and no one cares." We can get them all. And when we do this, when we change the contents of the filing cabinets, we change the programme, and, as it is the programme that drives the behaviour, if we change the programme, we automatically change the behaviour! Make sense?

Please understand me here, we don't choose this destructive behaviour, and we don't choose the fearful reactions, the negative thoughts – this is a filing cabinet! It can't choose, it can't decide, it can't think – it's a filing cabinet! The 'choosing' bit, the 'deciding' bit comes from upstairs, from the conscious mind. This lot down here, down in the basement - it just sits there in the drawers. It is not thinking, it is not choosing - it can't! And the behaviour, well, it just reacts automatically to the contents of the filing cabinets. So, if there are beliefs in there that say, "I am afraid," the behaviour will reflect that, and you will be anxious and nervous. If there are thoughts in there that say, "I love cake," you will want and desire cake, and you will find it almost impossible to resist the cake, despite being on a diet and your conscious mind telling you noisily to, "leave the cake alone!" Automatic behaviour, automatic responses and automatic reactions – they all come from the contents of the drawers. Want to change the behaviour? Then change the contents of the drawers!

So, how do we get them out? We go into a state of hypnosis. Hypnosis is just a deep state of relaxation. That's all it is. When we are tense, everything closes, everything gets tight. The opposite is true when we relax – we open. The deeper we relax, the more we open. If we imagine the conscious mind as a room, and this room has a secret door at the back, when we are tight, it is closed, and it is closed so tight we can't even see it, but when we relax, the door begins to open up. Through deep relaxation, we can imagine the room, we can open the door and we can go down the stairs into the basement, into our subconscious, and access our filing cabinets.

Let me explain about imagination. You used to have one when you were six, we all did. Children are incredibly imaginative and creative. The good news is, it is still there. It may be a bit rusty, but it's still there. (If you meditate, your imagination will already be good.) It is really quite easy to allow our imagination to come back out to play you know. Try this now...

Imagine a door. It's an arched, wooden door. This door is very beautifully carved, very ornate, a special door that leads to a beautiful garden.

Got a picture of that door in your mind now? See, easy isn't it? (If you haven't, practice until you can imagine the door.)

Now, for us to be able to sort our drawers out, we need to feel safe, and we need to feel powerful. The issue for many of us, is that we feel neither! So, we need to find a way to find that power. Let your imagination help you with this. Let's remember here, that this is *your* room, *your* cabinets, *you* made them and *you* own them. They belong to you. Imagine that you are a powerful wizard, or a magician. Or imagine that you are a powerful, rich Lord and this is your basement in your stately home – add in some servants who work for you, and order the servants to 'serve' you. Whatever and however you imagine it, you *must* be in charge and have full authority. (I see me as a Wizard when I am in here, with a wand and pointy hat - a bit like Merlin. I suddenly feel very powerful! I 'magic' the negative beliefs out of the drawers and into a fire. You might see yourself as Harry Potter, or something else. One of my clients imagined she had a dragon helping her to burn them up, another client had a load of Ninjas.) Your imagination is a wonderful tool – use it!

Let me explain just how powerful your imagination is. Scientists wanted to know how much the brain thinks is real and how much actually is – in other words, how much the brain is able to define which is fake - so they did some experiments.[21] They used a few professional athletes, and put monitors on the muscles in their legs and arms, and asked them to imagine that they were running in a race. There was a screen in front of them with a video playing a recording of a race. All the wires were hooked up to a computer and were there to measure any muscle activity in the athletes' body. Then they started the race on the video. The athletes were to imagine that they were on the starting line, and as the race started, they were to imagine that they were there, racing in it. Would it surprise you to know that the computer recorded every muscle firing in the exact, correct order that it would have done if the athlete had actually been in the race? Every muscle! And yet, none of them had actually moved a muscle - they were standing still. They were running the race only in their head, in their imagination, not in real life, but their brain thought they were actually there. Magic isn't it?

You may have heard people say, "What you think about, you bring about," or, "You are what you think." This is true. So, if we don't like the way we behave, react or respond, then we can change it, simply by using our imagination. We can imagine our self 'safe.' We can imagine our cabinets emptying of all the old beliefs. We can imagine creating new ones to replace them, and in so doing, we are changing our programme.

Memory.

Now, let's talk about memory. That's always a confusing one. Many people can't remember the detail of what happened to them when they were abused. It's either missing, or its foggy. This is okay. This is normal. Let me explain something about short and long term memory, and our 'memory filing system.'

Something happens, an event, an experience, and our mind creates a response to it. It creates a memory. This event pops into the short term memory. (The short term memory needs to be quite small, so that we can react quickly, remember easily, and not get too overloaded.) The new memory doesn't stay long in the short term memory. It only last about 15-30 seconds (just enough for us to absorb it), and then it goes through a little tunnel into the long term memory at the back - a huge storage area where all the memories are kept. That tunnel bit is where we process the memory, and we process it by understanding it. This is why it is so hard for us to remember things that we don't understand – they pop in and pop out again, without going into the long term memory. (This happens to me with algebra and equations! Languages is another. Repetition helps with this, as part of our brain will accept something it has heard or experienced before and create a memory from it to be filed.) Studies show that the deeper the level of processing, the more effective the entry into long term memory and its effective storage and later retrieval, suggesting that the quality of the memory is important and dependant on how it was processed or encoded.[22]

Imagine if we lived to be one hundred years' old how many memories would be in here – millions and billions! So, how do we find them? How do we find one single memory amongst all the trillions of memories in there? We file them, and this filing system, well, it needs to be a very sophisticated filing system indeed, or we won't be able to find anything. The brain uses something called 'priming' to do this. Priming is a kind of preparation. Let's imagine we have experienced a colour – say a flower that is pink. Our brain will have a filing cabinet for 'colour,' and it will have another filing cabinet for 'flowers.' The memory will go into both, and be linked with an association, so that when we think, 'pink flower' in future, our brain knows which cabinets to go to in the long term memory, in order to fetch the right memory back for us. Once it has found it, it brings it back through the tunnel, to the front, so that we can 'remember' it consciously. With me so far? (My psychology lecturers would have a fit at my description here of memory, but it is enough for our purposes here!) We can't possibly remember all of our memories consciously or our brain would crash, overload and blank out, so it kind of retrieves them one at a time, or in groups, and brings them back like that.

So, what happens when something happens for a first time, something that has never happened before? Where does the memory go if there is no preceding event that matches it? What happens if there is no filing cabinet for this event - it has never happened before and we have no idea where to file it or what to do with it? And what happens when we don't even know or understand what the event is? Nothing; nothing happens. The memory can't get filed. It is lost. It has nowhere to go. For us to file a memory, we need to first understand what it is. This is called 'processing.' Once it has been processed (understood), the brain prepares the correct filing cabinet for the memory to fit in. This is where the problem lies for children who have a sexual experience. There is no cabinet. A 'sexual experience' filing cabinet has not yet been created. And, there is no understanding of what this event is, no processing. The child does not know what this thing is that has happened to them. This event that just happened, it has no name. There is no understanding. A child of six, or seven, or eight, should have no understanding of sex. They do not know what it is, they do not understand what just happened, and they certainly don't know where to file it.

Now, let's imagine this enormous memory room with all of its cabinets, and with stacks of paper piled on top of loads of cabinets. All of these unfiled pages are events that we don't yet know where to put, memories without a place to go, so they sit there, unfiled. Now, imagine trying to go into this room and find a memory that has no drawer, and no filing system. It will be in that huge stack over there, amongst many others, so we can't find it, can't access it. Now, let's add a bit of denial into the mix. We want to believe that this thing didn't happen at all; we want to deny it. So, not only does it not get filed, it gets shoved into a box, with a lid, and the box is locked, and the key thrown away – like Pandora's Box, it stays hidden, out of the way, and it can stay there for decades. One day, out of the blue, some part of your inner self notices the box. The box starts to move forward out of the dark, blackness of the back of the room, and into the front. The box starts to open, and little broken bits of memories start to creep out. They are fragments, like pieces of a jigsaw. They form no picture, no image, nothing tangible, but we know it's uncomfortable. We know something is there – we just don't know what! Over time, those broken bits find their way into our subconscious and the subconscious wants us to figure it out, sort it out, deal with it, and then file it away as an event that once happened. So, it starts to give us those broken bits, in our dreams, in our behaviours, in our actions, and it feels awful. So, we avoid, distract, anaesthetise, repress, suppress and push down. We use drink, drugs, spending, relationships, work and chores, children and family, and anything else that we can find to distract our self with. We are experts at avoidance! I, myself, had 'A' level avoidance. In fact, I would go so far as to say I had a 'PHD in Avoidance!' The trouble is, the more we avoid, the more the subconscious pushes us to sort it out, but only when we are ready.

Our mind is very protective you know! It looks after us, and will only start to bring the box forward once it is sure that we are able to deal with it. When our inner self is convinced that we have developed enough wisdom, awareness, resilience, inner strength, honesty and trust - then it comes forward.

My memory was very good at keeping things back for many years. I was aware of some, but not all. As far as I was concerned, the things that I could recall were all in the past and I was no longer affected by it. I never thought about it, I never talked about it – I had pushed it all way down and out of sight. My first reaction to my own 'Pandora's Box' opening came when I was eighteen years old. I had gone to see a film in the cinema called 'Lipstick.'[23] I had no idea it was about rape, and I lasted about half an hour into the film before I ran out of there, literally, in a blind panic during the middle of the rape scene. I was crying and sobbing, I couldn't breathe, I felt sick, and I almost ran into the street and into the path of oncoming traffic I was in such a state! I had no idea why I had reacted like that! My partner who had paid for the tickets and had been forced to leave early, was furious, demanding an explanation, and I could not give him one. For days and weeks afterwards, I had flashbacks and nightmares, hot sweats and anxiety attacks, but gradually they subsided. I pushed it down, avoided and distracted, and, eventually, it all went away. From that point forward, I checked carefully what I watched and avoided all programmes with 'nasty stuff in them.' All good! My memories stayed nice and quiet for years, and then, one day, twenty years later, it came back. This time, I was older, wiser, stronger and more aware. This time I did not avoid, repress, suppress or distract. I sat with it, and I allowed it to surface. Pieces of the jigsaw came together, a picture began to form, and gradually all the sordid details came too. This time, I had a filing cabinet ready for them. This time, they could be processed and dealt with; then, finally, they could be let go. I worked on my beliefs, my memories, I pieced them together bit by painful bit. It was hard work, but it was worth it.

Now, I am free to watch what I want, when I want. I told you earlier, one of my favourite programmes is now 'Law and Order SVU'[24] – very different from all those years ago. I actually chose to watch that film 'Lipstick,'[25] that I referred to earlier, after I had done what I call my 'clearance work' just to see how I reacted after. I did not react. In fact, I no longer react or respond with fear to any programme or any story. I am no longer coming from that place because I have released all the emotions connected to the events, and, I have released all the old beliefs and formed new ones. I have literally reprogrammed myself. My memories of it are all there, but without emotional attachment, and without the painful, destructive beliefs about it, it is now just something that happened to me long ago.

I feel and think totally neutrally about it. I neither 'care' nor 'not care.' It simply 'was.'

This is not uncaring, it is neutral. Neutral is empowering, peaceful and safe. Neutral is liberating, and neutral is peace. It is that peace that I have tried to bring to others, and to help them get to where I am – into that neutrality.

I could not do what I do, helping other victims and survivors, if I reacted. I have to be neutral or I would be too affected by the horror stories I hear every day from my clients. And not only that, but a reactive life is a dramatic life, with rollercoaster living and loads of drama. I don't want that for me, and I don't want that for you.

Shall we go and sort those cabinets out then?

Exercise 5 – Clearing out the cabinets

Imagine a staircase deep in your mind. It has many steps going down and into your basement. Go down the stairs gently, and at the bottom of the stairs you will see a long, white corridor. Go right to the end of the corridor, and there, you will see a white door facing you. This door opens into your filing cabinet, archive room. Step into the room. Have a good look around you. Allow your imagination to run riot. Look at the floor – what is on it? It is carpet, floor tiles, rug, concrete, floor boards?

Look at the walls – are there any windows or pictures?

Look around the room – is there a fire place? Is it modern or old fashioned? Is it dark and dingy, dirty and grubby, or light, bright and clean?

Are there loads of cabinets or just a few? Are there any bookcases or shelves or boxes or hidden doors?

Get to know your room. Allow it to be however you see it - however you see it is just right. Don't try to correct it or change it.

Remember, you are in charge here; you are the Boss, the Magician, the Wizard. Take charge, take control. Now, order your cabinets to open. (They will all slide open immediately because you have ordered them to.)

Notice if it is tidy and organised, or jumbled and disorganised. This is okay, however it appears. It is representative of the state of your mind.

Now, notice the pages. Just A4 pieces of paper, all filed from the front to the back. Every page, every file, every folder represents all the different thoughts, all the different beliefs that you've ever had, going back over all time.

Some of these thoughts help you, serve you, support you, are good for you – and these are on white or light pages.

Some of these thoughts and beliefs do not serve you, do not support you, and these are on dark pages. They may be black, brown, grey or a dark colour, but they are not white.

I want you now to simply order out all of the dark pages. Just order them out! Just like Harry Potter they will fly out of the drawers and onto the floor, and they will form a pile of paper.

Let the pile be as big as it needs to be. It may come up to your knees, or your waist, or fill half the room, no matter. Just let it come.

Realise that each and every page on the floor is a thought or belief that has been working against you, creating fear and doubt.

Look for the thoughts and beliefs that are specific to you. Here are a few you will probably have . . .

I am not worthy, lovable, good enough, clean, nice.

I am invisible, no one notices me, I am not important, my voice is not heard, I am not heard, my opinions do not matter. I do not matter.

I am not safe. I am in danger. I am at risk.

I cannot trust people. I cannot trust myself. I cannot trust my judgement.

People are bad. My children are not safe.

I am disgusting, dirty, shameful and bad.

And so on . . .

Now, imagine a huge fire. It can be an open fireplace in the wall of the room, or a big incinerator in the corner of the room, or a fire-pit, or something else. Order all the beliefs on the floor to go into the fire, and watch them burn. They will burn quickly, easily, instantly. You are destroying, deleting, erasing and removing all of the negative beliefs. They are gone forever, permanently, deleted!

Once this is all done, I want you to imagine a table with a stack of blank, shiny, white paper on it. There is a pen there. You can use the pen or you can just 'magic' the words you want to appear onto the pages just with your imagination and thoughts. Now, create new beliefs that do serve you, that do support you. Make as many as you want and need.

Here are some suggestions . . .

I am safe. I trust myself. I trust my judgement. I trust my loved ones.

I am good enough, worthy, lovable. I deserve all good things. I am beautiful, amazing and strong. I am in control. I matter, my opinions matter, my voice matters. I am cared for, loved, supported. I am kind and good . . .

Make as many new beliefs as you want, and see them all going in the drawers.

Order the white ones at the back to come forward and reorganise themselves.

You can also imagine a photocopier in the room, and copy some of the more essential ones.

"I am safe" – make enough copies to have one in every drawer, right at the front, so that each time a cabinet is opened, knowing you are safe comes first.

Once you have finished, order the drawers to close and leave the archive filing room. Make your way back along the corridor, back upstairs, and bring your attention back to the room that you are in, opening your eyes gently.

Well done! You have just gone a long way to *Move Past the Past*.

You will need to do this exercise several times to clear out all the old, destructive beliefs, and to create new ones that help and support you. You will find that each time you go in there, the room changes. You may see more cabinets that were not there last time – this is okay. It is simply that your subconscious has held those ones back until you were ready to deal with them. You will also notice that it gets tidier, cleaner and brighter over time. It may also get more opulent, more luxurious, with carpets, rugs, pictures and the like appearing. Windows appear, the sun comes out and the room gets brighter. This room is your mind. As you clear out the negative stuff, your mind clears of clutter, of fear and of drama, and the way the room and cabinets appear reflect this.

Do the same thing with your memory room. You understand what sex is now, and have done for a long time. Imagine yourself going in there and ordering all the memories to go into the 'sex abuse' filing cabinet. Allow yourself to process and understand them this time, however uncomfortable and disgusting they are. We need to actively 'remember' what happened in order to make sense of them, and then they can simply be put away.

This work is so very important. Your beliefs are like an old, infected wound and they need to be healed. If I poke an open, septic, weeping wound, it's going to hurt, a lot! But if I open up the wound (painful as that is), and clean it out, and then stitch it up, it will heal. It may leave a scar, but over time, the scar will fade. We may always have that scar, depending on how deep the wound was, but it no longer hurts.

Throughout our lives, *we* are the open wound. We are constantly poked and prodded by triggers right into that wound and we react. *Rejected? Poke! Shouted at? Poke! Put down? Poke! Abandoned? Poke! Ignored? Poke!* You get the picture? But when we do this work to open it up and clean it out, it heals. Now poke me! I look at you calmly and quietly, and ask you simply,

"Why are you poking me?"

I no longer react.

To do this work, the work of cleaning out the wound, is painful, but it needs to be done. We do it by opening up the emotions, the trauma, the fear, the disgust and the rest, and we let it out. (We covered this in the last Chapter.) We also do it by opening up the beliefs in the subconscious, and letting them out. And we do it by opening up the memories, and letting them out, then refiling them into order. Add to this, the self-love that is building, the inner child work of healing 'Mini-Me' and the building of respect and safety, and we are nearly there. After all of this, we move onto emptying out the trauma and damage within the cellular structure – the physical body.

Let's go do that next – the physical body.

Chapter 6 - The Physical Body

Our body is an incredible healing machine. It is comprised of billions of cells, each one with its own lifespan. Each cell multiplies and divides during its lifespan, making new cells, and after time, the original cell dies. We see this on the surface of your body when you cut yourself - your skin will make new skin, and the cut heals. For most of us, our body was designed to be healthy. Disease and illness are therefore often created from the cells being out of balance, which happens when we are stressed, anxious, worried and vulnerable. The stress creates toxicity and pressure which is held within the cellular structure, making it very difficult for the cells to do their job.

Earlier, we discussed emotions that are stuck in the body. Each negative emotion is toxic to the body, weighing it down and creating discourse and disease. It is similar with the negative beliefs in the subconscious mind – they too, create toxicity and ultimately, ill health within the body. If I believe I am not safe, that belief will be sending signals into the body of 'danger.' The body will react accordingly, and push up adrenalin, the 'flight or fight' response. This, in turn, pushes up the thyroid and a whole chain of events happen biologically which results in illness within the physicality.

I mentioned within the Introduction of this book that many of my clients find their way to me initially because of health issues and not because of trauma. They present with Chronic Fatigue, Fibromyalgia, food intolerances and allergies, adrenal fatigue, thyroid problems and other physical symptoms, as well as mental health problems such as depression and panic attacks. Most have no clue that their health problem is directly related to their former abuse. In fact, most of them really struggle to 'get their head around' this concept at all!

Now, bear with me as this may sound very weird, but have an open mind on this. My belief, and many like me believe that the trauma from the sexual abuse is not only held within the emotions and the beliefs, but it is also held biologically within the cellular structure of the body, often at the point of impact. Many survivors of CSA have issues in the sexual and reproductive areas of their body – such as problems with periods, hormones, miscarriage or thrush. This is not a coincidence! Your body is literally holding onto the trauma within the cells of the body in the area of your abuse.

How does this work? Each cell has its own lifespan, and the memory of the trauma is held within the cell. As the cell multiplies and divides, it hands down the trauma to the next generation of cells, and so the trauma lives on within the body.

Let me give you some examples to help you understand this.

One of my clients has repeated mouth ulcers – her abuser attempted to force her to give him oral sex as a child. Another has endometriosis – she was raped as a child. Another client has issues with his rectum – he was anal raped as a child. For me, I suffered all my life with my periods, my womb and my ovaries from the age of twelve. I experienced three miscarriages over the next twenty years, and also had polyps, cervical issues, endometriosis, all of which resulted in several surgeries and other medical procedures to try to fix them. Nothing worked. Every month I would menstruate and every month the colour would drain from my face within minutes of my period starting. The pain would begin immediately and I would have to take extremely strong pain killers and go to bed, sometimes for days.

I also experienced repeated throat issues, from laryngitis to tonsillitis from the age of eight upwards, as well as ear infections, along with both my ear drums perforating in adulthood several times. My ears were holding the trauma of physical assaults of dozens (or maybe hundreds) of hard slaps across the side of my head by my mother, not to mention the trauma of being screamed at, with words of abuse and cruelty. This verbal abuse would include things like, "I wish you had never been born," and "I hate you," or, "You filthy bitch," or, "You are a bad, bad girl and you deserve nothing!" My throat was holding my 'un-screamed screams', along with my 'unspoken words of secrecy.'

I believe that all of these physical issues were as a direct result of the trauma within the cellular structure of my body – trauma that was held in several different areas. My sexual region was holding the trauma of my sexual abuse, and resulted in problems in my womb and reproductive system and my head area was holding trauma within the ENT region (ears, nose and throat). Little wonder my ears and throat weren't happy, or that they continued to give me problems for most of my adult life, and little wonder my womb was traumatised either.

Many of my clients experience ENT issues and many more experience fatigue, anxiety, panic attacks, thyroid problems and even skin issues. Someone make your skin crawl when you were a child? Hmm, and now you suffer with psoriasis, eczema or skin allergies. Coincidence? I think not!

These physical problems are the *symptom* not the *cause*. It is this that we must understand and accept. Yes, I can see your raised eyebrow here in scepticism – that's okay. Let me be a little more specific.

At the time I did my 'clearance work' on myself (releasing my trauma) I was currently awaiting an operation for a full hysterectomy. During my release work, I visualised all of the trauma in my vagina, cervix and ovaries leaving me. I focused on the abuse, and then on the three miscarriages. I felt a massive shift within my body physically, as well as emotionally. Within three days of releasing this trauma I had the first 'normal' period of my life. "Is this what a normal period feels like to others?" I asked myself, "Can it be this simple, this easy? Have I healed myself by simply imagining the trauma leaving me?"

The answer was a loud 'yes'! A few days later I received the appointment letter from the hospital with a date for my hysterectomy surgery for a few weeks' later. I asked for a postponement, which I was given. The following month I had another normal period, and another. By the sixth month I felt confident enough to cancel my hysterectomy. It was the right decision. I still have 'all my bits' many years later and have never had any issues with my periods since. By facing my trauma and healing myself, I have avoided unnecessary major surgery, which is an enormous thing. I did the same work on my throat, visualising and releasing the secrecy, the invisible 'gag' and the 'inability to speak up.' I did the same on my ears, releasing the trauma there too, from both the physical abuse from the slaps as well as the verbal abuse from the words. My womb and throat is now fine, and my ears are getting there. They are still sensitive, and, according to the specialists, I have much scar tissue in the ear canals and on the ear drums, which is why my ears are taking a little longer to heal. I have no doubt that they will get there.

It is a similar story with many of my clients. After releasing the trauma in the body, emotions and mind, the majority of their physical symptoms ease, reduce or go completely. My clients with reactions to food begin to reintroduce foods that they were previously unable to tolerate. Those with CFS start to feel their energy return, and gradually they are able to return to normal life. Panic attacks go, depression lifts, joints and muscles get stronger, and the body begins to heal on a cellular level. It's absolutely essential to do this work on your body, because if we don't, the statistics are frightening! The ACE study suggests strongly that we are at a far higher risk of illness and early death than those that have not experienced our traumas, and it needs to be sorted!

Let's try to understand the ACE study a little more, and what it evidenced regarding childhood abuse and ill-health in later life. The ACE[26] study was one of the largest scientific research studies of its kind, with over 17,000 Americans participating. The focus was to analyse the relationship between childhood trauma and the risk of physical and mental illness later in adulthood. Over the course of a decade, the results demonstrated a strong relationship between the level of traumatic stress in childhood and poor physical, mental and behavioural outcomes later in life.[27]

The study showed that the higher your ACE score, the higher your risk of health issues in adulthood, including ischemic heart disease, cancer, chronic lung disease, skeletal fractures, and liver disease. It proved that early stress is a strong factor for developing the following health problems: Cardiovascular disease, Cancer, Heart attacks, High blood pressure, Stroke, Diabetes, Weight gain (especially abdominal fat), Exhaustion, Reduced Growth Hormone Levels, Compromised immune function and Bone loss.

The study also found that those with an ACE score of 6 or more had their life expectancy reduced by approximately twenty years.[28] Now, I know this is all scary stuff about health, but forewarned is forearmed as they say. I don't know about you, but I'm not best pleased that my lifespan has been cut short by twenty years! I want to do something about it, as I am sure you do! So, first off, you need to find your score. As I said earlier, understanding and awareness are the keys here.

(The referencing with all the detail on these studies is at the end of the book.)[29] [30]

To find your ACE score you need to answer a series of questions. . .[31]

While you were growing up, during your first 18 years of life:

1. Did a parent or other adult in the household often or very often . . .

Swear at you, insult you, put you down, or humiliate you or act in a way that made you afraid that you might be physically hurt?

If yes enter 1 _____

2. Did a parent or other adult in the household often or very often... Push, grab, slap, or throw something at you or ever hit you so hard that you had marks or were injured?

If yes enter 1 _____

3. Did an adult person at least 5 years older than you ever . . .

Touch or fondle you or have you touch their body in a sexual way or attempt or actually have oral, anal, or vaginal intercourse with you?

If yes enter 1 _____

4. Did you often or very often feel that . . .

No one in your family loved you or thought you were important or special?

Or . . .

Your family didn't look out for each other, feel close to each other, or support each other?

If yes enter 1 _____

5. Did you often or very often feel that . . .

You didn't have enough to eat, had to wear dirty clothes, and had no one to protect you?

Or . . .

Your parents were too drunk or high to take care of you or take you to the doctor if you needed it?

If yes enter 1 _____

6. Were your parents ever separated or divorced?

If yes enter 1 _____

7. Was your mother or stepmother:

Often or very often . . . pushed, grabbed, slapped, or had something thrown at her?

Or . . .

Sometimes, often, or very often . . . kicked, bitten, hit with a fist, or hit with something hard?

Or . . .

Ever repeatedly hit at least a few minutes or threatened with a gun or knife?

If yes enter 1 _____

8. Did you live with anyone who was a problem drinker or alcoholic or who used street drugs?

If yes enter 1 _____

9. Was a household member depressed or mentally ill, or did a household member attempt suicide?

If yes enter 1 _____

10. Did a household member go to prison?

If yes enter 1 _____

Now add up your "Yes" answers: _____ (This is your ACE Score.)

So, how was that for you? Mine is 8. Anything over 4 is dodgy in terms of its effects on our physical health. The official findings[32] of the study found that those of us with high ACE scores would likely have some or all of these:

- Alcoholism and alcohol abuse

- Chronic obstructive pulmonary disease

- Depression

- Foetal death

- Health-related quality of life

- Illicit drug use

- Ischemic heart disease

- Liver disease

- Poor work performance

- Financial stress

- Risk for intimate partner violence

- Multiple sexual partners

- Sexually transmitted diseases

- Smoking

- Suicide attempts

- Unintended pregnancies

- Early initiation of smoking

- Early initiation of sexual activity

- Adolescent pregnancy

- Risk for sexual violence

- Poor academic achievement

Blimey, no wonder we may die early! It's a long list isn't it? That being said, we discussed a lot of this in Chapter 1, so we don't need to go over it again. By now, we have done a lot of work to *Move Past the Past,* and this includes being able to change the outcome of our health. A healed body is a healthy body! Throughout this book, we have already healed our inner child, and we have healed our heart, then we healed and cleared our emotions and our thoughts, so now it's just the physical trauma in the body that is left.

It isn't just me that believes trauma is held in the body and results in the manifestation of illness. There are prolific writings and writers on the subject. The main ones I rate are Louise Hay[33] (loads of books from 1984 to present day – too many to list, but all good! I have put the link to her website in the note); The Journey by Brandon Bays[34]; The Emotion Code by Dr Bradley Nelson.[35]

All of these writers show you ways to release trauma from the body, and it is their teachings, amongst others, that have inspired me to heal myself, and to add some of their methods into my own hypnotherapy practice in order to heal others.

So, now it is time for us to do the same work on the body that we have already done on the emotions, the heart, the child and the mind. Let's go fix the physical body!

Exercise 6 – Healing the Physical Body

As always, make sure your phone is off so that you can be undisturbed. Allow yourself to relax and go back to the garden. This is your safe place, your healing place. Set your intention to release all trauma from the body and ask your subconscious and physical body to work with you.

Imagine in the garden is a full length mirror on a golden stand. Go and stand in front of it and look closely. Ask your body to show you where it hurts, where it is holding pain. Allow your mind, memory and emotions to work together as a team to help you. Start from the top of your head and work your way down your body, as if you are doing a scan – just as if you are seeing your body with X-ray eyes. Notice where it hurts, where it is darker, or where there are blocks.

Now, go into each block, each shadow, each trauma, and one by one, ask them to go. They will begin to find their way out. Work on each one until you feel they have been released.

Open your heart to all the love you have inside, and pour that love into the damaged area, with the intention that you are setting it free and healing it. Visualise it healing.

You may want to go into the lake during or after this to help your body to relax, be free and feel safe.

When you have done what you can, come back from the garden, into the room and back to conscious awareness.

You will need to do this exercise several times until the body has fully released all of its' trauma.

If you need help to do this, on my website you will find audio downloads which are guided meditation sessions to heal your body.

http://www.juliepoolehypnotherapy.co.uk/product/body-can-heal-part-1-29-mins/

http://www.juliepoolehypnotherapy.co.uk/product/body-can-heal-part-2-26-mins/

It may also help you to read some of the recommended books on the subject, or to download audio books and meditations. There is lots of help out there. Go with the ones that you feel drawn to, whether they be scientific, medical ones, or more alternative, holistic ones. Do what you need to do to heal your body. When I came to do mine, I had already read loads of these so I had a head start in terms of my own understanding and awareness. I am also deeply spiritually conscious, and used this to add to my healing. I firmly believe that I have now extended my life span by releasing this trauma in my body. I can't prove it, yet, but I'm expecting to be living into my seventies now, or even my eighties, rather than popping my clogs in my early sixties!

At the end of the day, what have we got to lose? Precisely!

I've talked a little in this Chapter about books, downloads and help that is out there. The last Chapter of this book will discuss other support that may be needed, and will show you some different options and possibilities that are available, but before we get to that, there is one last part of the jigsaw that we need to examine – that of 'Revictimisation.'

Chapter 7 -
Revictimisation

Many of us who were abused as children go on to be abused again later, and sometimes, again and again! This is called 'Revictimisation.'[36] It is so common to be re-abused that scientists have even studied the phenomena, and it is they who have labelled it, 'Revictimisation.'

Sexual revictimisation occurs when a survivor of sexual abuse or rape during childhood is victimised again during adulthood.[37] CSA survivors are between 2 and 11 times more likely to experience adult assault compared to non-victims.[38] In addition to this, there is growing evidence that repeated traumatic experiences, such as revictimisation, may be more likely than a single traumatic incident to damage the person more deeply as they are cumulative in nature.[39] I call this the 'boxer effect.' If a boxer is punched so hard that he hits the deck in 'Round 1,' he can get back up again. However, by 'Round 15,' and punch after punch, he is finding it really difficult to get back up again. It is the same with us. One assault was bad. Somehow we find a way to get back up again, but when it happens again, and again, we find it harder and harder to get back up. This is the cumulative effect of multiple abuses, often across decades.

I too, experienced revictimisation. I was abused as a child before the age of ten, both physically, mentally and sexually. At the age of thirteen I was sexually molested by an acquaintance of my step-mother who was giving me a lift, and took me instead, down a lane and molested me in the car. I was able to fight him off, but it left me severely traumatised. I told my step-mother but wasn't believed, because he was 'such a nice man' and I was being 'ridiculous.' At the age of sixteen I was sexually molested again, this time by a shop keeper when I had gone in to buy milk just before closing. He was locking up at the time, and came behind me at the counter, groping me and pushing me into the counter from behind. Somehow, I also managed to fight him off and ran out of there. This time, I reported it to the police. I was interviewed, gave a statement and he was given a caution. I was told by both the police and my family to put it behind me and forget all about it. A few months later, still at the age of sixteen, and, within a week of leaving school, I was thrown out of home by my mother and told to never come back. I was highly vulnerable, and, after a period of sofa-surfing, I went into an abusive, violent relationship where I was abused on multiple levels for the next three years by my partner. Three years later, at the age of twenty I found the strength to leave the abusive relationship and gradually, in time, I began dating again. On my second date, I was date-raped. It was just a few months after I had left my abusive partner! I don't know how, but somehow I managed to get past that one too, or so I thought!

Over the next few months life got better. I developed new friends, and even started a little job. I moved into a nice flat and I was happy. Weirdly, this is when I suddenly crashed. I had never experienced depression before, or panic attacks. The despair and panic became overwhelming and, as far as I was concerned, had come completely out of the nowhere. I wasn't sleeping or eating properly, I became kind of dazed and not really 'present' and I was constantly afraid, even though I was safer and more stable than I had ever been before. It made no sense to me at all and I felt even more confused and alone. It gradually got worse, and eventually, I went to my GP in desperation and asked for a referral to a Psychiatrist for help because I truly thought I was going insane. I attended one session and was diagnosed with PTSD (post-traumatic stress disorder). The Psychiatrist explained what it was, and, although I didn't really understand it, the part that I did understand was that he said that I was allowed to feel like this, and that it was a normal reaction to what I had been through (and I hadn't told him half of it!). That was good enough for me! I took that to mean that I wasn't ill, that what I was feeling was normal and that it would pass in time. Just coming twenty-one years of age, I decided that I didn't need to go back to see him again. After all, he was a Psychiatrist, and they were for mentally ill people, and as I clearly wasn't 'insane,' just suffering from some 'shock thing,' I didn't need to go! Ah, the logic and ignorance of youth! And, what a huge wasted opportunity!

My symptoms were very typical for PTSD, which, by its very name is a 'post' reaction, as in 'after'. Our trauma tends to begin to only come out *only after* the trauma has ended, hence my PTSD building over a six month period after my last abuse had ended. It only began to be displayed once I had become safe for the first time in my life. Sadly, I did not accept the help on offer at the time, and, as a result I continued to suffer with PTSD for the next sixteen years, with deep bouts of depression and anxiety. I also continued to add to the trauma with bad decision making and reactivity due to the unhealed trauma, meaning that there was more to deal with once I was ready for help.

Many young adults do exactly the same as I did, unable to process or deal with their trauma - they simply do not have the cognitive or emotional awareness at such a young age. Those rare ones that can and do, are able to begin to deal with their trauma, and to avoid adding to it. One of my clients, Molly, (not her real name), is one of them. When she was only twenty-two years old, she was offered help from a '12 Step Programme.' Through this, she was able to face her past and deal with much of her trauma. Molly has bravely agreed to share her story with us. She is a forty-nine year old American living abroad and is a high school teacher.

Molly's Story

I have had a number of incidents that seem to have cumulatively had an effect. I was molested by my father early in life – sometime before five years old when he and my mum divorced and likely as young as six months – I had a bladder infection at that age that I suspect was due to sexual abuse. Certainly a bit later (again before age five) he molested me further. At around seven years old I was chased and attacked by a group of teenage boys – I do not have clear memories of the attack itself, but it was sexual in nature. They left me naked in an outbuilding afterwards and threw my clothes up on the roof.

My step-father sexually abused me later – around ten to twelve years of age. My mom was a prescription pill addict, so she was not able to notice what was happening to me. She was a perfectionist and I now understand that she was depressed and found it difficult to cope with life. This meant that she was often angry and I was left feeling unacceptable and as though I was not good enough, no matter what I did.

I have a natural curiosity and desire to seek challenges, enjoy social company, and have a talent for leading others. However, the abuse shut these qualities down. I did not feel any safety in the world and came to believe that I deserved what happened to me. I rejected men who were good to me, and was attracted to men who abandoned me, betrayed me, lied to me – I didn't feel that I deserved men who would treat me with respect. I accepted disrespectful behaviour from friends and was often bullied at school.

I developed an eating disorder (mostly anorexia and bulimia) at around age nineteen, and found recovery from this at the age of twenty-two through the 12 step programme, and as an inpatient in a long-term recovery home/treatment centre. I had used food as an overeater for most of my childhood, but had not been conscious of it because I was thin until my late teens.

I did not go to university until I was twenty-four (after I was in the first stage of recovering from my eating disorder and the sexual abuse), even though I had high grades in high school – I didn't believe I was smart enough.

My health declined from around age twenty-six – I developed recurrent vaginal and urinary infections, and after repeated antibiotics, I developed chronic fatigue, and latterly migraine headaches. I was depressed enough as a teenager to seriously consider suicide. I was depressed again off and on to varying degrees after this, and suicidal on some occasions. This peaked last year and coincided with further health problems – I am not sure to what extent the depression was caused by my other health problems and an inability to take in vitamins due to a poor digestion, and how much of my poor health was due to the depression – they seem to be mutually occurring.

I first saw a Psychologist at the age of eleven because I was not sleeping. I now know that this was because my stepfather was abusing me most nights, but I had blocked this out of my daytime conscious thoughts until I recovered from my eating disorder. I never told my mom as a result, so she just knew I was having sleeping troubles. I saw her for a couple of sessions only. It helped my sleep somewhat – all I remember is that she taught me relaxation techniques.

I got involved in a church at age sixteen. This helped me to feel a sense of belonging that I lacked at home, but I also felt like an outsider since I did not believe what the others believed. I just wanted somewhere to go where I felt accepted.

I tried therapy again at around age twenty-one, when my eating disorder was at its peak. This had no effect, because I did not stop the bingeing, starving, purging or over-exercising, so I never dealt with what was underneath it. This was traditional talk therapy, but I had no conscious feeling, just misery softened by my eating behaviour.

I tried church again around the same time (a different church group), but it didn't help at all.

It was only when I found the 12 steps of 'Overeaters Anonymous,' that I felt my first sense of a solution. This helped me to stop the compulsive eating behaviours, so that I could start dealing with what was underneath. I discovered a sense of true belonging, but also a sense of purpose in helping others. The 12 steps helped me also to uncover the parts of my personality that had adapted to survive the abuse, and to work on changing these to healthier responses and relationships. I also found a concept of spirituality that really fit for me, whereas church had not done this for me.

Around the same time, I went into inpatient treatment for my eating disorder. In the treatment centre, I had regular group and individual therapy, which was mostly Jungian/Gestalt. This really helped me to externalise a lot of the pain and anger of the abuse in order to move through some of it. I was able to start having healthier relationships and to date again (I had been completely celibate for the years of my eating disorder – I had given up on men).

At age forty-eight (about a year ago), I became increasingly depressed and anxious, due to a toxic work environment that triggered feelings of disrespect from the childhood abuse. It came to a point when I was concerned about being able to continue working and functioning. I was more suicidal than I had ever been before, and was feeling in serious danger. I lost an opportunity for a much better job as a result, which sent me lower. At this point, I was referred to Julie for help. I had never tried hypnotherapy before, but I was willing to try anything to get better.

It was an immediate relief from my first session. Julie showed great insight and compassion about my feelings and showed genuine understanding of how my trauma history had led me to this point. This was significant for me in being able to trust her in the hypnotherapy portion of the sessions and relax into these. I think this meant that the hypnotherapy was able to be effective. The sessions felt/feel extremely personalised – the imagery that she uses is directly relevant to what I am working on. In the sessions, she leads me through visualisations of various rooms and outdoor places. For example, in one session, she 'took' me to a room with lots of filing cabinets and we worked on throwing away the files that were no longer serving me, in terms of old beliefs that were holding me back and leading me into unhealthy situations. It is amazing to me how I can be both completely present in myself, but also completely present in these visualisations. I always feel really peaceful afterwards. They have helped me to change behaviours and beliefs.

I have now achieved a new job, which I hope is going to be much better than my previous one. I have also improved my relationship with my husband – I was feeling very distant from him and the sessions helped me to be stronger in my own boundaries with him and to feel that I had a right to do that. Now I feel much closer to him, because I am able to be honest with him about my feelings and how he impacts me. I have also been able to stand up to my boss, who was so disrespectful to me and was a bully – I told him that it was not acceptable for him to speak to me that way and he changed his behaviour towards me after this. I also started to tell him when I disagreed with him. I have been able to set boundaries with other people in my life also – both personal and professional. Sadly, my sister has all but stopped speaking to me, partly as a result of this, but I am not willing to accept what she sees as acceptable behaviour towards me. This feels really sad.

My health is also improving. I have changed the supplements that I take, but I feel that the internal changes I have made as a result of hypnotherapy have coincided with finding the right physical treatments to help me, plus that the internal emotional and spiritual changes are also allowing my body to heal and the physical treatments to have a greater impact.

I still have further to go. Although I achieved a new job that I am excited about, I also did not have the courage to pursue some other employment options that would have fit more with where I want to be. I still have old ideas to work through and fears to release, but it is improving.

The sessions are between an hour and 90 minutes (occasionally 105 minutes). I have been working with Julie for just over a year, and I "see" her every 2-3 weeks, although initially I was seeing her weekly.

Although I gained an enormous amount of help and personal change from the 12 steps and from inpatient treatment – these relieved a significant layer of the damage from my past – hypnotherapy has healed old beliefs that were still holding me back. I can now see that the crisis of the past year has allowed me to access the greater healing that I have found in hypnotherapy, which was beyond what other therapies and approaches were able to offer me, because of how it has allowed me to access aspects of my subconscious mind. I cannot emphasise enough how important the trust with Julie has allowed for this – the hypnotherapy on its own without this trust would not have been effective. This level of trust has arisen from her willingness to share her own experience of healing from trauma and from her consistent respect and support, even when I have not been able to make the changes she has suggested sometimes when I have not been ready for them.

I would like to think that the universe would have offered me another alternative if I had not pursued hypnotherapy, but without the changes that it has brought me, I'm not sure how much longer I could have stopped myself from serious self-harm and even death. I might not have stayed married to my husband, and I might well still be in the same horrible, abusive job, as I would not have had the mental strength to pursue other opportunities and to walk through the fear to quit my job a year before the contract finished.

I do not know how much longer I will need hypnotherapy, but I have made significant improvements. I still have further work to do. I have certainly come to a place where the effects of the trauma of sexual abuse and emotional rejection/neglect/abuse from my mother have significantly healed and do not impact my day to day life in the ways that it did previously.

I hope in five years to be living in a place where I really want to be – I still allowed my husband's desires to supersede what my heart was telling me when I made the decision to take this job. I see myself having more fulfilling, more intimate relationships with people I want to have in my life, a greater sense of community and belonging in the world, making more time for activities beyond work (which I tend to rely on to fill me up). I believe that hypnotherapy has put me on a path to be able to see these goals, never mind the potential to be able to fulfil them. It has opened my mind and my heart to alternative ways of seeing the world and my place in it."

I am sure that you are as moved by Molly's story as I have been whilst I have been working with her via skype. Her story is one of revictimisation and PTSD on a grand scale. She has worked so hard to get to where she is now, and I am honoured to be part of that healing. Molly is also typical, from what we have learned, in not believing she was smart enough to go to university, and in developing an eating disorder, both of which were helped when she joined 'Overeaters Anonymous.' This help, at the age of twenty-two was crucial to her wellbeing, and to her future.

Molly's story sees the typical abuse pattern of self-destruction, with suicidal tendencies, depression and the acceptance of disrespect and abusive relationships, not just at home but also at work, and with family and friends. Molly naturally feels sad that her sister is not currently in her life, but this is not unusual. You will find that many relationships change or end once your boundaries and self-respect are in place and you are in a place of strength within yourself. It is sad, but it is often inevitable. My parents are still alive and I choose to be estranged from both of them, and have been for some years. I also let go of several friends when I understood that they were toxic to me, removing them from my life in one way or another within a year of my healing. It left a hole in my life, but one that I filled with new friends who do respect me, and strengthened relationships with those friends that remained. My 'family' is now not only my children, but also my close friends. Blood is not thicker than water you know, particularly when that blood consistently judges and hurts you. There may come a time for you too, when you choose to end relationships that have been in your life for years. My suggestion to you is that this action is as a last resort, and only after you have tried all else, but when your new boundaries have failed with these people, and they continue to damage you, removing them from your life may be the only way to protect you. Remember your priority is to you first and foremost, always!

In terms of revictimisation, Molly has been in a stable relationship for over twenty years now, which has helped to strengthen her. It is possible that she was only able to develop and build this healthy, stable relationship because she had received treatment for her PTSD several years earlier. Whilst she freely admits that she has let her husband get away with too much over those years due to her own weak boundaries, she has not seen a repeat of abusive relationships since her early-twenties. However, she has remained vulnerable to bullying at work as well as disrespect from friends and acquaintances, all of which she is currently working on, and all of which are improving.

Another client, we shall call him Ian (not his real name), also experienced revictimisation. Ian is a forty-four year old electrician. He had been experiencing suicidal thoughts for over ten years and came to me for help on the recommendation of a friend. This is his story.

Ian's Story

"It was like I had this big, gaping hole inside me all my life. I felt stunted, restricted, lost! I'd tried to fill it with spirituality, and it had helped, but nothing had ever fixed it. I have two adult children from a former relationship, and I love them enormously, and they fill my hole a little, but I find our relationship challenging. I want to be the best dad I can be, but I struggle to do the right thing, say the right thing, be there for them, or be enough. I always feel like I've let them down, failed them. It was the same with my partner, really. I've been with my partner for

the last fourteen years, and she puts up with a lot. I know I'm really reactive, and very defensive. I find it difficult to let her in, even though I do trust her and I love her totally, I just find it so hard. Bit like life really. I wake up every day with this heaviness, this dread, deep inside my chest. It feels crushing, suffocating, and the fear that is with it, well, it's just terrifying. I live every day of my life constantly terrified. A lot of the time this affects my ability to work, to provide and even to function. I hate myself, despise myself and feel I am a total failure. I live with this every day of my life and after a while, it just overwhelms me and I crash into a deep depression. I know I'm a nightmare to live with! She deserves so much better than me and I have no idea why she puts up with me. She's a saint!

I was sexually abused by a family member when I was seven or eight. For the next ten years I felt dirty, disgusting, shameful, hateful, confused, afraid and lost. I never told anyone or talked about it – it was this huge, dirty secret that was locked inside me. Through my teens I turned to spirituality, and found my way, at around eighteen years of age, to India, and into an Ashram. All I wanted to do was to heal, and to fill this big, dirty hole in that was deep inside of me. Instead, what I got, was more of the same. My 'spiritual master' targeted me for 'special healing,' and I trusted him totally. I trusted him the first time he pulled my trousers down and groped my testicles and anus, and I trusted him the second time, even though it felt bad, awful, sickening and terrifying. He told me that he was 'healing my damaged parts' with his molestation, and I was so trusting because he was this big, famous, spiritual leader. It was the most unbelievably confusing thing! My inner self was disgusted and appalled, and yet, at the same time, because of who he was, I couldn't believe that he was doing anything wrong. I left the Ashram and tried to put it behind me. I lived with it for years, a decade or more, then one day, I came across someone else within the spiritual community who said the same thing had happened to him by the same man, and he said that it had happened to hundreds, if not thousands, of others. They were all male, all aged eighteen to twenty-two and all had a history of childhood sexual abuse. They had also been molested in the same way by this same man in the Ashram. My friend told me that the police were even doing an investigation into him for sexual crimes, but then he died, and the investigation died too. For the first time, my confusion left, and I realised I had been abused again. I felt sick to the stomach, and even more lost than I had before. That was when it got really bad, the depression, and the heaviness in my chest every morning on waking, and each year, it just seemed to get worse.

Eventually, I hit rock bottom, and I don't know why, but one day I told my partner everything. The relief was incredible! After her, I told my family, and eventually, I went to a counsellor. She was alright, I guess. She helped me talk about it, which was good, but nothing else happened. I knew I needed more, and then my partner found out about Julie. I knew straight away that she was the right person to work with from the first five minutes of our session on skype. She seemed to 'get me' and there was absolutely no judgement. It helped a lot that she told me that she'd been through it too, and she shared information when it was appropriate to help me understand myself. There was a deep, intrinsic connection of trust and support, and I was able, over the course of our sessions together, to finally fill my hole. We worked on my self-hate and got rid of that by opening my heart to my own love, and we released all the shame and disgust. I cried a lot during these sessions, but they were healing, releasing tears and felt good to get it out. We did some inner child work too, to heal little me. I didn't even know I had a 'Mini-Me'! My 'Mini-Me' was a cat, and it took a while, but we finally found trust in each other. Almost from the beginning of my sessions with Julie, I felt calmer, less defensive, more open and more willing to discuss, rather than react. Julie taught me how to communicate, to share my feelings and express myself. She also gave me tools which I use all the time. I saw her for four months every week and then it felt right to stop for a while, to let it all sink in and process.

My relationships with my children are now really good, and my relationship with my partner is amazing. I know I have more to do, and when I am ready, I will work with Julie again, but for now, I just feel good for the first time in my life, and that's where I need to be right now."

We can see from Ian's story that he was re-abused in his late teens, which compounded his self-hatred and shame. As time went by, the cumulative effect took its toll on his health, wellbeing and relationships. As a man, being often unable to work and provide for his family due to depression also hit hard, leaving him feeling even more of a failure. Emotionally, feeling fear and dread constantly is also very difficult. Men are conditioned from childhood to 'provide for their family' and to be 'fearless and brave.' Ian felt neither, just lost and scared, and so felt less of a man, which damaged his self-esteem even further.

Dealing with emotions for both men and women is difficult. "Boys don't cry" is a saying many of us have heard, along with, "Big girls don't cry," or, "be brave and strong." We are taught from a young age that crying is weak, and 'toughing it out' is strong. One of the first things I work on with my clients is to break down this conditioning and free the emotional barrier to allow the emotions to express themselves. Big girls and big boys do, indeed cry, and they tend to cry a lot when they work with me! I tell them, as they apologise through their tears, "Don't apologise, I make people cry for a living!" handing them the box of tissues that is always at the ready. Eventually the tears stop, and under them, is a relief and a peace that is welcome and needed.

We can see from their very open and honest stories, that Molly and Ian have had repeated thoughts of suicide throughout their adult lives, finding life extremely hard work and often not wanting to continue. This is often the case for us. Those that have not experienced the incredible dread and despair that we often live with daily, cannot possibly understand the effort it is for many of us to simply exist whilst we carry such pain. I understand completely how despair can become overwhelming and, like Molly and Ian, I had lived with suicidal thoughts that came and went for many years too. For those of you who have not really ever felt this, and for the partners who feel it is the ultimate betrayal that your spouse would abandon you and/or your children through such destruction, let me try to explain what it feels like for us.

There were times, prior to my own healing, when I was completely convinced that I was a useless, inadequate, unwanted, rejected failure and life would never, ever get any better. This heavy dread that we live with, coupled with the almost constant fear is debilitating. The self-hatred is palpable, and it turns inwards, along with the hatred at and of life. We hate life so vehemently, why would we want to live? These emotions are powerful, and incredibly destructive. This level of fear and hate destroys, inside and out, everything that is good. It blinds us to anything positive - all we can see and feel is our pain. At these times, when I felt like this, I was completely unable to see that my children needed me, or what it would do to them to be abandoned so violently and absolutely by their mother's suicide. All I knew was that I wanted the suffering to stop, and it wasn't stopping. The dread and pain were there every day. All I could see was that I was

better off out of it and my children were better off without me –
after all, I was a toxic, dangerous mess and they deserved more. I
believed that I was saving them from me by removing myself from
the equation and saving me from the pain by embracing death. I
was very wrong! The damage to a child of a parents suicide is
indescribable, not to mention the wonderful years I would have
missed out on, and I thank God that I never succeeded in my acts
of ultimate destruction.

Oftentimes, it is the suicidal thoughts that get stronger and
louder that bring us to our healing. Being at rock bottom can be
the push that we need to finally deal with our pain and to seek the
help that we so desperately need. Personally, I hit my 'rock
bottom' at the age of thirty-seven. It was through this particular
pit of despair and darkness that a part of me somewhere woke up
to the destruction, the fear, and the hatred, and it was this rock
bottom that finally pushed me to sort it out. I stopped avoiding, I
stopped hiding, I stopped looking for my peace outside of myself
with distracting, toxic relationships and the 'save the world' jobs,
and I focused, instead, on saving myself. This is when I finally
faced up to the sexual abuse from my childhood, the damage of the
re-abuse through my teens and to the date-rape. I was ready!
Gradually, slowly, I began to face it and in so doing, I began to
heal. It took me a few years to pull it all together. I began to put
myself first, building my sense of self, respect, boundaries and
self-love. I released the toxicity and damage within my thoughts

and beliefs, emotions and body, and I worked with and on my inner child. When all of that was done, I put myself into therapy with a specialist counsellor. It was a hard, tough, emotional journey, but through it, I finally found a sense of peace.

Many of my clients are in their late-thirties to late-forties when they come to me. It is at this stage of our life that we have often developed a sense of awareness deep enough to realise that we need to face our demons, and, with help, to have the tools and capability to process our past.

Ian's story shows us how he too, finally found his peace. His depression is gone, his suicidal thoughts a thing of the past, and his life better than ever. Throughout his ups and downs, like Molly, somehow he managed to hang on to his relationship, although at times, only just!

So, what is it like to be the partner of an abuse victim/survivor? I asked Ian's partner to share with us her thoughts - this is her story. We shall call her Sarah (not her real name). Sarah is a forty year old Market Researcher and has been living with Ian for the last fourteen years.

Sarah's story (A partner's perspective.)

"When I met Ian it was love at first sight! We met at a counselling course as we were both considering a career in therapy at the time. We had so much in common – same philosophy on life, both spiritually conscious, same values, it was perfect. The first six months were 'heaven on earth' and we were blissfully happy. And then the trouble began... As the honeymoon period wore off, the real Ian emerged. This guy nosedived into a deep depression for no apparent reason. He just wasn't the man I knew! This Ian was reactive, incredibly moody, needy and clingy at times, then distant and withdrawn at other times. He was often childlike, unable to act like an adult, take responsibility or deal with life. His emotional needs often took over and there seemed to be no room for my own. Living with his obsessiveness was another thing that was hard – it's almost OCD and was quite challenging. He had regular angry outbursts that left me confused and walking on egg shells, particularly in the mornings. (It was normal for him to wake up in a terrible mood and stay that way for half the day. I had no idea why.) It was exhausting. He was always sorry afterwards, and very loving and apologetic. I knew he meant it, but I constantly lived on edge waiting for the next outburst or over-reaction. It could be something so small, and rows would come out of the blue, and then escalate like you wouldn't believe! I often questioned why I was putting myself through it, but I stayed, living on an emotional rollercoaster for most of the next twelve years. At

times, over the years, I've had to be a buffer between him and his children when he's had his unreasonable outbursts, and mediate and calm things down between them. I think the children have been the glue that's held him together, and probably why he never attempted suicide, although I know he's thought about it often.

Many times I nearly walked, and psychologically I think I constantly had one foot in the door and one foot ready to go. I packed my bags many times, but somehow, we managed to always find a way through. I think I was able to deal with it because I am a strong person in myself. Don't get me wrong, I had my times when I reacted to his outbursts. I lost the plot with him now and then, and got really angry and despairing on more than one occasion – dealing with his emotional turbulence was just such hard work! But I deeply loved the man I knew was there, underneath all those outbursts. In between those, his caring, loving, humorous and passionate qualities shone out. Yes, there is no doubt that we truly loved each other, but if I had not been as emotionally and mentally strong as I am, I could never have coped with his moods, or with the constant ups and downs.

Just over a year ago, he had another mini breakdown. It was then that he finally told me everything. He opened up and shared with me his abusive past, and it transformed our relationship almost instantly. I'd had no idea! Once he'd told me, he then told his family, and everything was out in the open. We became closer than ever, more intimate and more trusting after his revelations.

His outbursts made sense to me at last, and my own confusion left. It was then that he decided to get help, and went to a local counsellor. It lasted about eight weeks but made little difference. She listened to him, allowed him to talk, which was great, but she didn't give him any tools to deal with anything. He stopped going and I wasn't sure where the journey would go next, because he clearly needed something deeper. It was then that a friend of mine told me that she had been working with Julie for a while and suggested that Ian see her, so I set it up. It was exactly what Ian needed. Julie 'got' him in a way that the other counsellor hadn't, and he was able to trust her almost immediately. As Ian began working with her, the transformation was almost instant. After each session he was calm, almost serene, and almost overnight, became a joy to be with. He grew up almost straight away, no longer reacting or having any outbursts, but calmly being able to talk and discuss things like adults. His defensiveness, which was previously absolute, just melted away. He is also now able to be supportive of me and my own needs, which is new! And the morning moods have gone away too. It's just lovely. Ian worked with Julie for about four months, and then he took a break (which he's still on) to consolidate the work they had done so far. He is aware that there is more to be done, and I am sure he will return to work with Julie in the future, but when he is ready, and that's fine with me. His obsessiveness is still there, but it's much calmer than it was before, but I think there is more to do.

From my perspective, as a partner, I would say that you need to make a decision quite early on whether you are going to stay for the long haul or run, and if you are going to stay, to get some support. I think the partner holds the victim together, and it's exhausting and draining. You need help to be able to do this, and I think without my own knowledge and awareness of this stuff from my own therapy and training, I'd never have coped. I had a strong enough foundation to be able to weather the storms, but they were tough! You need a real inner core of strength, which I had. All in all, I thank God that he finally found the strength to tell me and to work with Julie to sort it out. It truly has transformed our relationship. I am happier now and we are stronger as a couple than we have ever been, and I look forward to each day with Ian."

It is testament to Sarah's own resilience and strength that their relationship survived those turbulent years. She now has a wonderful, loving relationship that is more equal, more balanced and more peaceful than she could ever have imagined. She is absolutely right in terms of needing support as a partner of an abuse victim. We are hard work and even harder to live with until we are healed, and even then, we have our scars and our vulnerabilities that make us harder to be with at times. That being said, we are also incredibly loving, kind, supportive and beautiful people. We are strong and caring, and we tend to be incredibly non-judgemental, which is a wonderful quality. We are also very loyal, valuing these normal qualities within a relationship that many others take for granted. Trust is everything to us, and to feel enough. All we really need is to feel safe, to feel loved and to be respected. It really isn't that hard, or that much, and blimey, we deserve it after all we have been through. It is only the partner who can decide if we are worth the trouble of the extra work that our baggage often brings, and, if they can't handle it, then that's okay.

Strong, loving relationships like Ian and Sarah's, or Molly and her husband, are beautiful, but not all relationships are like this, as I am sure you know. Trust me on this when I say, it is better to be single than to be in a toxic relationship. If you are, I hope that through this healing, in time you will find the strength to leave. This will then be the time to learn to first have a relationship with yourself before you go into a relationship with another. All of the 12 Step Programmes recommend that you spend a year single before trying to date. This is for exactly that reason. I am not suggesting here that you leave a healthy relationship, God no! Only that you not fear being single, as it can be the most liberating, building time that enhances your future, both for yourself and for your future relationships.

The childhood abuse and the repeated pattern of multiple abuses is horrifically damaging to us. So, why does this happen, this repetition of abuse? Psychologists and Psychiatrists suggest that the pattern of revictimisation is due to the underlying cognitive beliefs that we are not good enough and that we deserve what we get. However, it goes much deeper than that.

Studies suggest that an underlying factor to revictimisation is PTSD (post-traumatic stress disorder).

Another factor is desensitisation - this is where the previous abuse may actually desensitise the survivor to real threats and decrease the likelihood that the person will respond to perceived danger.[40] This desensitisation results in increasing difficulty in distinguishing between true alarms and learned alarms.[41] The perpetrator, in turn, may recognize the victim's inability to accurately assess risk and act upon this vulnerability.

Dissociation is another factor that may increase the risk of revictimisation because sexual predators may learn to recognize such confusion or distractibility as signs of a woman's vulnerability and be more likely to attack such women.[42] The organisation 'Mind' states that "Dissociation is one way the mind copes with too much stress, such as during a traumatic event. The word dissociation can be used in different ways but it usually describes an experience where you feel disconnected in some way from the world around you or from yourself."[43] So, we disassociate from the reality around us, staying instead inside ourselves, and may often create a fantasy of what we want something to be, rather than what actually is. Some people actually have the sensation of leaving their body during the abuse. I know I did. This is a common reaction and is a way of not feeling what's going on by not being there. This disassociation is one of the ways that we have learned to cope, and links strongly into how we can be drawn into abusive relationships – we just don't see the signals or the warning signs, seeing what we want to see instead.

In addition to these contributory factors, we can add in the difficulties that many survivors have with mental health, drugs and alcohol, all of which will inhibit judgement as well as increase known risk factors. I think that learned behaviour is part of it too, especially with survivors of grooming. When we are trained to be sexual beings from such a young age, it can become part of our natural character, and we can find that we unknowingly send out the wrong signals, opening ourselves up subconsciously to abuse from those that recognise the victim within us. Add to that our faulty 'abusive/nice men radar' and we are hugely at risk of repeating the patterns.

I, like many of us, experienced multiple revictimisation situations. The evidence shows us that even when we think we are healed, we can slip back into old patterns, particularly at times of high vulnerability. Our 'danger radar' is switched off and the old expectations of abuse return subconsciously. We are then more at risk to abuse at these times of vulnerability as we have poorer judgement than normal. To combat this, we need to ensure that we put higher levels of protection in place at times of high vulnerability in order to make sure that we are safe. Awareness is the key, so if you are going through a hard time with a particular issue, be aware that your vulnerability is higher, and therefore your judgement and radar is probably lower. With that awareness in place consciously, you are more likely to be able to protect yourself.

This pattern of revictimisation is intense and deep. It covers multiple layers and we often need an expert to help us to break them and uncover them all. We will talk about this and what help is out there in the next Chapter – The Need for Support.

Chapter 8 - The Need for Support

I cannot emphasise enough how important support is, and the right type of support. There are many out there – spiritual, religious, self-help books, DVDs and audios, support groups, psychological, medical, nutritional, CAMS (complimentary alternative medicines), family, friends, nature, animals, exercise . . . use all or some, but use them! Let's look at some of them now.

We are spiritual beings you know. When this part of us feels fulfilled, it enriches and supports us. If you feel that you need to tap into your, or 'A' higher power, look into what spiritual or religious organisations and groups are out there and go along to a few and try them out. See if anything fits. One size does not fit all, and each area of support needs to feel a perfect fit for you.

Support Groups offer specific help, and there are absolutely loads. Just do a simple 'Google' search on sexual abuse support and you will come up with hundreds of pages of suggestions. Also, look at other support groups for some of your reactors, like our Molly, who found the 12 step programme. Whether it is food, alcohol, sex, gambling or something else – there is a 12 step programme for that. Be open to these groups. There can be incredible support just being with other survivors who will understand you like no one else will.

Psychological help - There are a myriad of Counsellors, Psychotherapists, Psychoanalysts, Psychologists and Psychiatrists out there. Like all walks of life, there are the good ones and the not so good ones. My suggestion is that you find one that specialises in childhood sexual abuse, and an analyst who understands and works with, 'transactional analysis' therapy. This type of therapy focuses on what is called the 'drama triangle' of 'victim, persecutor, rescuer,' and, 'adult, child, parent,' which many of us are stuck in and need to be freed from. You need to feel a connection with this person, and a trust in them. Go for one or two sessions, and if it doesn't feel right, leave, but don't give up. Keep looking until you find the right one.

I worked with CRASAC – 'Cornwall Rape and Sexual Abuse Centre.' I believe most counties in the UK have something similar. They offer free counselling and support specifically for sexual abuse, and I found them wonderful.

CAMS (complimentary, alternative medicines) offer a huge variety of different things that can give you support. Hypnotherapy is actually classed as a CAM and was huge for me, obviously. Another enormously beneficial thing is meditation. Then there are the healers, from reflexology to reiki, acupuncture to Bowen Technique. There are crystal healers and colour healers, and the list goes on, and on, and on. Be open and try the ones that you feel drawn to. I used hypnotherapy, Reiki, massage and meditation as my starting points, and each one I found to be hugely helpful. (I eventually became a Reiki Master myself.) I have also had colour and crystal healing, Indian head massage, full body massage and aromatherapy, simply because learning to be touched in a safe way on my skin went a long way to helping me to heal, not to mention the self-love I was doing by prioritising and pampering me.

Family - crucial! All of my clients have either had supportive parents or a loving, supportive husband/wife/partner when they were going through their healing. Each of them reported that they could not have done it without them. (In fact, you could – I did, but I agree, it is much easier with that support.) The most important thing with parents and partners as your support is that they allow you to cry, feel, rant, express and deal with whatever is coming up. The last thing you need is your partner trying to comfort you and telling you not to cry, or trying to get you to 'pull yourself together!' Some may even suggest you stop your therapy and go back to the way you were before. Hmm. Warning bells here folks! If they do that, you need to ask yourself if they truly love you, or if they are just scared for you. If it's that they are scared, you need to explain to them that it may be a bit of a rollercoaster whilst you are going through the healing and release work, but they are not to panic, not to take it personally and definitely not try to fix you. Explain that you may be more sensitive and more vulnerable at this time, and that you may be more reactive for a while, but that it will calm down once it's all out.

For your part, understand that this is really hard on your loved ones. They will feel helpless, useless and panicked a lot of the time as they see you go through it. No one likes to see someone they love in pain, and the instinct is to make it go away and fix it. Explain to them that they can't – all they can do is to hold your hand and be there for you, to allow you to talk, feel and cry, and to listen. That's really all they need to do, is to listen.

What about after you have done the work? What can you and your partner expect? What will be different?

For a start, your boundaries will change. From their perspective, the goal posts have moved and they will be bemused. Suddenly you are disagreeing, whereas before you would have capitulated. Suddenly you are saying no, whereas before you would have said yes. You are now being more assertive and more independent, and it's all changing! Help them to understand, and be patient with them while they get their head around the new rules. Be patient, but be assertive. This is now the 'new you' – the 'real you' – the 'you' that you would have been without the abuse! You are quite a different person during and after your healing work, and your partner will need time to adapt.

If they can't or won't adapt, you may need to let them go from your life. This is the sad reality, but it may happen. Many partners choose a 'victim' as their husband/wife because they are a 'rescuer.' Now, the thing is with rescuers, they need someone to rescue! Once you have rescued you, their job is kind of redundant, and they may not like it! They may try to put you back into victim mode so that they can get back to their comfort zone of rescuer. This is their stuff, not yours. You could try couples therapy to help them to change too, but if it doesn't work, you may need to let them go. In time, they will find someone new to rescue, so that their patterns can keep repeating, if that is what they need to do. And, in time, you too will find someone new – someone that appreciates and loves the real, whole, independent, strong you just the way you are!

Friends – where appropriate, tell your friends what you are going through and why. Ask for their support, care and time. You will be able to tell your friends things that you may not tell your partner or parents, so this extra support is essential. Be aware that this can be draining on them, and don't lean too heavily on them or they may bend. (Some of my friends were bent half double by the time my therapy finished, bless them! Since that time, I have made sure that I have bent double for them too.) A real friendship is give and take, and mutual, two-way support. Like the partners who don't support you, those 'friends' who are not there for you are not true friends. You may begin to see 'who your real friends are' through this time, and exit or distance some of them from your life, as I did. Don't worry if this happens. Life hates a void and once you create one, it will move new friends into the gap.

Nature – the healing energy of nature is incredible. Walking by water can calm you in an instant. Being near trees, a walk through the woods listening to the birds singing and the rustling of leaves will also heal and calm. Being out in a park, on the moors, or anywhere in nature helps to rebalance, regenerate and heal. Use it as much as you can. It will make the healing process so much easier.

Animals are another area of support that should not be underestimated. I have a pet dog called Oscar, a two year old King Charles Cavalier that I hand-picked out of the litter at just three weeks old. He is my best pal, my best friend and the love of my life! I don't know where I'd be without him. I talk to him when I am confused, I talk to him when I am lost, I share with him my rants and raves when I'm 'in a mood' and he listens to every word with a "Woof" and the obligatory 'lick to make it all better.' He gets me out of the house and interacting with the world, even when I'm not in the mood, and he brings contact with other human beings who always stop to pet him and chat to me when we are out. Dog people always seem to talk to other dog people! Love from a pet is completely unconditional and we can take and learn a lot from them.

Exercise is another key area of support. We know that when we exercise the body releases natural endorphins into the system, which are the body's own natural pain killers and relaxers. Most people report that they feel so much better after a run, or after the gym, or a swim, or a walk. Find what works for you and what is enjoyable, and use it to help you heal.

These, to me, are the key supports that you will need. It's not realistic for me to list all the different types of support that are out there for you, there are just too many, but I have given you a few to ponder on. The most important thing for you to know is that it is there, but this part is for you to do. Only you can decide what support you need, for how long, and in what way. Only you can pick the right one, and 'feel' if it feels right.

Now, I do need to manage expectations here. This journey is not easy, but I promise you that it is worth it. You may go through an emotional rollercoaster when you begin this journey, and it can be exhausting, time consuming and often expensive with therapies and healings. You will 'stop/start' a fair bit too, doing bits at a time, leaving it, and coming back to it. Your past pain tends to come up in layers, and you may think that it's all done, then out of the blue, another layer, like an onion, shows itself. I began my journey in 2001. I was 'stop/start' for the next three years, but by 2004 I felt it was all done, that I was free and that it was all behind me. I was right, but I was wrong too! I had released, realised and understood everything that I could *at the time*. Over the next eight years I continued to grow, strengthen and develop, and then in 2011, during some 'Emotion Code' release work that I was doing with a therapist friend over some day-to-day stuff, up came another layer which I wasn't expecting, still related to the abuse that I thought I had cleared. I was quite surprised, but I was able to clear it quite quickly and easily. I realised that I had not been ready for that deeper bit back then, and the fact that it was coming now meant that I was clearly ready now, so I just went with it.

You will need to have an open mind to your layers too. You will clear what you are able to clear at the time, and you may decide, "That's enough for me," and, if you do, that's totally fine. You may never come back to do any more, and, as long as you feel happy and settled, then you have achieved what you need to achieve. Equally, don't feel upset or disappointed if another layer shows itself further down the line. It may, or it may not surface, but if it does, try to go with the flow and trust that your subconscious is bringing this to conscious awareness now because you are ready.

Trust also, that it needs to be done. Your inner self really does know best, and the more that you can trust it to lead and guide you, so much the better.

Maybe some of us, or maybe none of us ever truly heal from it all, and yes, scars are there. Maybe they will always be there. It is clear that sometimes those scars start to bleed again and we need to do a bit more work. But, by the end of each bit that you clear, you will find a freedom and a peace that you never felt possible. It may be that you feel, as I did in 2004, that you have now found your total peace once you finish the first layer, but believe me, that was just the beginning for me! I would say that my peace is tenfold now to what it was in 2004, it just keeps growing! It may be that there is only one layer for you to clear, or you may be like me, an onion, with multiple layers to clear. Whichever it is, it's okay.

So, what have we learned throughout this book? We have, I hope, understood why we do the things we do and why we react the way we react, and that those reactions and things are quite normal responses created from our abuse – *that they were not our fault!* This has enabled a deeper understanding and forgiveness of our self and our past, enabling old wounds to begin to heal. We have also understood and worked on the concept of self-love, and we have carried out exercises to open us up to that love. We have met with 'Mini-Me' and healed our inner child. We have released all those powerful emotions that were throughout the body physically, releasing the damage within the cellular structure. We have changed our thinking and beliefs, and burned all the old, destructive ones, and we have learned about revictimisation and how to protect our self. Not much then!

So, how are your reactions now? Do you feel more neutral now when you think back to the abuse? Does it feel calmer, safer and easier? I do hope so.

Like me, you may feel that you want to move on from this work we have done here afterwards, and into psychological therapy. I found it impossible to do that work on myself because I am too close. I needed someone to help me to see how this abuse had warped my view of the world, of men, of relationships and of people. I needed help to understand how it had affected my behaviour, my thinking and my actions. Look at your own patterns of behaviour and identify what works against you, and find the right therapist to work with to break them.

Now we have come to the end of the journey that I have taken you on throughout this book. You have read it all, and, hopefully, you have understood it all. I hope that you can see the way that it all pulls together – that each element, on its own won't do it, but as a whole, holistically, it does. Now you know the whole, go back to the exercises and work through them again and again until it all feels clear, open and easy. Once all that is done, go and find yourself the right therapist to work with on your behaviour, if you feel you need to and want to.

By doing this work, you are leaving the chaos and the drama behind you. You are walking away from trouble, grief and stress. You are no longer reacting, you are no longer destructive.

Remember a while back I talked about your train? Well, with each of those exercises that you have done, you have uncoupled a carriage that was blocking your way forward. You are now in the front carriage of that train, and the train has just pulled into the station called 'Peace.' You are now free to step off the 'Chaos train' and jump onto a different train!

The work that we have done here, within this book, will go a long way to help you to break free of the pattern of abuse and revictimisation, and help you to make the changes that you seek to free yourself from your past.

You can finally *Move Past the Past* and into your peace.

You are already on that journey to peace or you wouldn't still be here, reading the last page of this book. Thank you for staying with me through these pages, and I want to say this to each and every one of you . . .

You are the most incredible person that you will ever know, and you absolutely deserve to be free of your past. You have the strength, the courage and the determination to face your demons and release them, and you are ready to 'Move Past the Past.'

Welcome to peace!

Now, you can enjoy this journey that we call life!

Congratulations and well done!

The End

Bibliography / Endnotes

[1] http://www.medscape.com/viewarticle/824023

[2] https://www.ncbi.nlm.nih.gov/pubmed/11888413

[3] http://mendingthesoul.org/research-and-resources/research-andarticles/abuseisdevastating/

[4] Pérez-Fuentes G, Olfson M, Villegas L, Morcillo C, Wang S, Blanco C. Prevalence and Correlates of Child Sexual Abuse: A National Study. Comprehensive psychiatry. 2013; 54(1):16-27. doi:10.1016

[5] Radford, L, Corral, S, Bradley, C, Fisher, H, Bassett, C, Howat, N, & Collishaw, S. Child abuse and neglect in the UK today. NSPCC. 2011.

[6] http://arkofhopeforchildren.org/child-abuse/child-abuse-statistics-info

[7] Felitti, V. J., Anda, R. F., Nordenberg, D., Williamson, D. F., Spitz, A. M., Edwards, V., & Marks, J. S. (1998). Relationship of childhood abuse and household dysfunction to many of the leading causes of death in adults: The Adverse Childhood Experiences (ACE) Study. American journal of preventive medicine, 14(4), 245-258.

[8] Saunders, B.E., Kilpatrick, D.G., Hanson, R.F., Resnick, H.S., & Walker, M. E. (1999). Prevalence, case characteristics, and long-term psychological correlates of child rape among women: A national survey. Child Maltreatment, 4, 187-200.

[9] Finkelhor, D., Ormrod, R.K. & Turner, H.A. (2010). Poly-victimization in a national sample of children & youth. American Journal of Preventive Medicine.

[10] Walker, E.A. Gelfand, A., Katon, W.J., Koss, M.P, Con Korff, M., Bernstien, D., et al. (1999). Medical and psychiatric symptoms in women with children and sexual abuse. Psychosomatic Medicine, 54, 658-664.

[11] Fuemmeler, B. F., Dedert, E., McClernon, F. J., & Beckham, J. C. (2009). Adverse childhood events are associated with obesity and disordered eating: Results from a U.S. population-based survey of young adults. Journal of Traumatic Stress, 22, 329 – 333.

[12] Rohde, P, Ichikawa, L., Simon, G, Ludman, E., Linde, J. Jeffery, R & Operskalski, B(2008).Associations of child sexual and physical abuse with obesity and depression in middle-age women. Child Abuse & Neglect, 32, 878-887.

[13] Sedlak, A.J., Mettenburg, J., Basena, M., Petta, I., McPherson, K., Greene, A., and Li, S. (2010). Fourth National Incidence Study of Child Abuse and Neglect (NIS–4): Report to Congress, Executive Summary. Washington, DC: U.S. Department of Health and Human Services, Administration for Children and Families.

[14] Finkelhor, D. (2012). Characteristics of crimes against juveniles. Durham, NH: Crimes against Children Research Center.

[15] Elliott, M., Browne, K., & Kilcoyne, J. (1995). Child sexual abuse prevention: What offenders tell us. Child Abuse & Neglect, 5, 579-594.

[16] London, K., Bruck, M., Ceci, S., & Shuman, D. (2003) Disclosure of child sexual abuse: What does the research tell us about the ways that children tell? Psychology, Public Policy, and Law, 11(1), 194-226.

[17] Leeb, R., Lewis, T., & Zolotor, A. J. (2011). A review of physical and mental health consequences of child abuse and neglect and implications for practice. American Journal of Lifestyle Medicine, 5(5), 454-468.

[18] Prevent Child Abuse America (2003). Recognizing child abuse: What parents should know. Chicago, IL. Retrieved 5-31- 2013 from www.preventchildabuse.org.

[19] Girardet, R. G., Lahoti, S., Howard, L. A., Fajman, N. N., Sawyer, M. K., Driebe, E. M., et al. (2009). Epidemiology of sexually transmitted infections in suspected child victims of sexual assault. Pediatrics, 124, 79-84.

[20] https://www.nbc.com/law-and-order-special-victims-unit

[21] http://jn.physiology.org/content/112/12/3219

[22] Craik F & Lockheart R (1972) Levels of Processing: A Framework for Memory Research. Journal of Verbal Learning and Verbal Behaviour. 11, 671-684

[23] Lipstick (1976) Paramount Pictures

[24] https://www.nbc.com/law-and-order-special-victims-unit

[25] Lipstick (1976) Paramount Pictures

[26] Felitti, V. J., Anda, R. F., Nordenberg, D., Williamson, D. F., Spitz, A. M., Edwards, V., & Marks, J. S. (1998). Relationship of childhood abuse and household dysfunction to many of the leading causes of death in adults: The Adverse Childhood Experiences (ACE) Study. American journal of preventive medicine, 14(4), 245-258.

[27] http://www.americasangel.org/research/adverse-childhood-experiences-ace-study/

[28] https://www.scientificamerican.com/article/childhood-adverse-event-life-expectancy-abuse-mortality/

[29] https://www.cdc.gov/violenceprevention/childmaltreatment/consequences

[30] Felitti, V. J., Anda, R. F., Nordenberg, D., Williamson, D. F., Spitz, A. M., Edwards, V. & Marks, J. S. (1998). Relationship of childhood abuse and household dysfunction to many of the leading causes of death in adults: The Adverse Childhood Experiences (ACE) Study. American journal of preventive medicine, 14(4), 245-258.

[31] http://www.acestudy.org/the-ace-score.html

[32] https://www.cdc.gov/violenceprevention/acestudy/about.html

[33] http://www.louisehay.com/

[34] The Journey: A Practical Guide to Healing Your life and Setting Yourself Free (1999) Brandon Bays

[35] The Emotion Code (2007) Bradley Nelson. Wellness Unmasked Publishing.

[36] Messman-Moore, T. L., & Long, P. J. (2003). The role of childhood sexual abuse sequelae in the sexual revictimization of women: An empirical review and theoretical reformulation. Clinical psychology review, 23(4), 537-571.

[37] Messman, T. L., & Long, P. J. (1996). Child sexual abuse and its relationship to revictimization in adult women: a review. Clinical Psychology Review, 16(5), 397–420.

Messman-Moore, T. L., & Long, P. J. (2000). Child sexual abuse and revictimization in the form of adult sexual abuse, adult physical abuse, and adult psychological maltreatment. Journal of Interpersonal Violence, 15(5), 489–502.

[38] Fergusson, D. M., Horwood, L. J., & Lynskey, M. T. (1997). Childhood sexual abuse, adolescent sexual behaviors and sexual revictimization. Child Abuse and Neglect, 21(8), 789–802.

[39] Follette, V. M., Polusny, M. A., Bechtle, A. E., & Naugle, A. E. (1996). Cumulative trauma: the impact of child sexual abuse, adult sexual assault, and spouse abuse. Journal of Traumatic Stress, 9, 25–35.

[40] Messman-Moore, T. L., & Long, P. J. (2003). The role of childhood sexual abuse sequelae in the sexual revictimization of women: An empirical review and theoretical reformulation. Clinical psychology review, 23(4), 537-571.

[41] Barlow, D. H. (2002). Anxiety and its disorders: the nature and treatment of anxiety and panic (2nd ed.). New York: Guilford Press.

[42] Cloitre, M., Cohen, L. R., & Scarvalone, P. (2002). Understanding revictimization among childhood sexual abuse survivors: An interpersonal schema approach. Journal of Cognitive Psychotherapy: An International Quarterly, 16(1), 91–112.

[43] https://www.mind.org.uk/information-support/types-of-mental-health-problems/dissociative-disorders/

Manufactured by Amazon.ca
Bolton, ON

12714137R00092